Taking the Long Way Home

Taking the Long Way Home

Ted Staunton

Kids Can Press Ltd., Toronto

Kids Can Press Ltd. acknowledges with appreciation the assistance of the Canada Council and the Ontario Arts Council in the production of this book.

Canadian Cataloguing in Publication Data

Staunton, Ted, 1956-
Taking the long way home

ISBN 1-55074-089-X

I. Title.

PS8587.T38T3 1992 jC813'.54 C92-093535-4
PZ7.S73Ta 1992

Kids Can Press Ltd.
585½ Bloor Street West
Toronto, Ontario, Canada
M6G 1K5

Printed and bound in Canada
Edited by Charis Wahl
Cover design by N.R. Jackson
Interior design by Pixel Graphics Inc.

92 0 9 8 7 6 5 4 3 2 1

To Melanie and Will

Chapter One

THERE WAS THE LONG WAY HOME AND THE short way home. If you went the long way, you left my friend Maggie's, went all the way down Maple Avenue, then up Riverview to the corner and back along Greenapple Street to my place. It was no sweat if you were on your bike — and if you were going to get in eight tons of trouble from your parents, it was never far enough — but it felt like a million miles if it was supper time and you were walking. That was the time for the short way. All you had to do was cross the street from Maggie's to the Fenways', cut through their backyard, hop the fence, and you were behind our garage.

Cinchy. Except that the Fenways had this little dog that was always sitting in their living-room window, and whenever anyone even looked over there it would go nuts, yapping and bouncing up and down like a hairy little hamburger on springs. Then grouchy Mr. Fenway would nail you as you whipped past their back door. I practically never took the short way, no matter how hungry I was. Maggie took it all the time from my place and somehow she never got caught. Well, she was Maggie and I was me. People like her can do stuff like that and people like me can't. Maybe that's why we were friends.

So when Maggie started complaining the Saturday afternoon we were going out with her mom, it didn't really bug me.

"Jeeeeez, Cyril, hurry up." I *was* hurrying, with all my library books, too. "Why didn't you take the short way?"

"He'll catch me," I panted. My breath clouded up like I was Cyril the Human Smokestack, and I was wondering what a burp would look like. For only October it sure was cold. My mom had even made me wear my toque.

"He only catches you because the dog starts yapping, Cyril." Maggie jumped off the front porch and headed for their van in the driveway. They had to get a van after Maggie's mom had twins.

"Yeah, so?" I said. I tried to pull my hands up into my jacket sleeves but it was tough with all the books. Maggie was busy biting a fingernail. Maybe her hands weren't cold.

"So, the dog sits in the front window, Cyril. He only sees you when you start from my house. When you come from your place he can't see you till you're practically on the street."

"Oh. Yeah." I felt like a dwork. Why hadn't I thought of that? Because there were people like Maggie and people like me. But that didn't make me feel any less dworky.

Maggie swung the big back hatch open on the van. Inside was a folded-up double baby carriage. "Hey," I said, "what's that for?"

"The twins are coming with us. My dad has to do some incredibly important emergency dentist work on one of his patients, so my mom has to bring them."

"What!" I screeched. "Awwwwwwwww —" A dragon-sized cloud shot out of my mouth. Just hearing the twins were coming made my toes curl up.

"Tough beans," Maggie snapped. "Now, quick, before my mom comes out. I've got more contests to enter." She stopped biting a finger long enough to pull out a little roll of papers in a rubber band. She stuffed them in my jacket pocket.

"Hey! Get out!" I said, and jumped back, my hands still full of books.

"Oh, Cyril, there's only five entries for each one. And in case you forgot, you promised. Remember?" Maggie sniffed.

"Yeah, I promised, *if* you helped me with — "

The front door of the house opened and Maggie's mom called to her. Maggie ran back inside. I dumped my library books beside the baby carriage. Maggie's books were already there. As Maggie and her mom came out of the house with the twins, I stuck my hand in my pocket. It felt like she'd stuffed the telephone book in there. I sighed. Maggie had secretly turned into a contest maniac, and I was helping her fill in entry forms. She was supposed to be helping me as a trade but she hadn't done anything yet. She said she was still thinking about my problem. I wasn't so sure. All I ever saw her do these days was bite her nails.

I wasn't sure about this afternoon, either. The last time I'd gone somewhere with the twins they'd overflowed their diapers and stunk up their clothes, and then they wouldn't stop crying. Gross tomatoes.

Maggie and her mom strapped the babies in their car seats in the middle of the van, then Maggie and I slid into the seat at the very back. The twins were bundled up like squirmy blue sausage rolls.

"They better not wreck everything," I whispered. I'd been waiting for this all week.

"It won't be bad, Cyril." Maggie didn't sound like she meant it, but she didn't like it when anybody but her complained about the twins. "Besides, I don't even know why you're getting a haircut."

It sounded as if she was teasing. "Oh yeah," I said back. "Well, I don't even know why *you're* getting one."

And I didn't, either. Maggie's birthday had been a little while back and she'd asked her parents for a new haircut. Maggie never cared about haircuts before, and *I* didn't have time to care why she did now. Because, see, she gave me the idea to ask for one, too. I had an excellent reason but I wasn't telling anybody. So I said, "Anyway, they'll squawk all the time we're at the library." The Readathon was on at school, and Maggie and I were leading in our class.

"They will not, Cyril. They'll sleep. Won't they, Mom?" Maggie had to shout a little. Her mom was way up front in the driver's seat.

"We can only hope, kids." She smiled and started the van.

I loved riding way up high in the van. It smelled new and it was about a million times nicer than our crummy old cars. When I bugged my parents to get one, they said we didn't need it and we couldn't afford one. I guessed that meant Maggie was rich, but when I asked her she said she didn't think so because her parents had been complaining about how much everything cost ever since they moved from Greenapple Street.

By the time we got to the mall I wasn't thinking about any of that stuff; I wasn't even worried about the twins. All I wanted was my haircut. All the way there, Maggie and I talked about the kind we'd get. I was allowed to get any kind I wanted as long as my dad could recognize me, but I couldn't make up my mind. Neither could Maggie. That just made it better. It didn't even bug me when Maggie and her mom started arguing in the freezing parking lot because the baby carriage wouldn't unfold.

Maggie and I ran ahead of her mom and the twins. Except for our house, the mall was my favourite place in the whole world. I liked it even better than Maggie's van. All the lights and the new stuff and the people and the food smells from Nosher's Nook — pizza and Chinese and fries with ketchup and vinegar. It was excellent.

When we got to the door of the haircut place we were grinning like crazy. The Hair Today shop had all these mirrors and bright lights and TV screens. The whole place was checkered black and white. Everybody in there was a high-schooler for sure, and they all seemed to be moving to the music video pounding out of the TVs. And the hair! Every wild haircut I'd ever seen was in there somewhere. There were sweeps and slashes, patterns, shaved sides, flat tops, long hair, short hair, almost no hair at all.

Everybody looked so cool, I knew they'd laugh at me for sure. All at once I could feel my toes curling again and I wanted to be home in the kitchen, getting a plain old haircut from my mom, like usual. Maybe I could just ask for a trim, sort of.

"C'mon Cyril." Maggie tugged at my sleeve as her mom came up. "What are you waiting for? Let's go!"

But there was nowhere to go. You had to give your name to this guy with purple streaks in his hair and then wait for your turn. He said it would be at least an hour. My toes started to uncurl, but Maggie groaned and her mom's shoulders went all saggy. The twins were bawling almost as loud as the TVs. They didn't like the video, I guess.

Maggie said we could go play video games for an hour, but her mom said no, we weren't going to wait.

"Then come back for us," Maggie said. "We'll be all right."

"No. You're too young to be left alone at a mall."

"*We are not*," said Maggie. "Are we, Cyril?"

Before I could talk Maggie's mom said, "I'm not going to stand here and argue with you, Maggie."

She breathed hard out her nose and her mouth got all pinched in. The twins cranked up the bawling. "The twins can't take it here and I don't have it in me to walk them for an hour. I'm sorry but we'll have to try to come back later." She didn't sound sorry, she sounded mad.

Maggie opened her mouth but her mom said, "Maggie!" I pretended to be all interested in the rakes outside the hardware store. A minute later we were heading for the van. Secretly I was glad, but the way Maggie looked, I wouldn't have told her for anything. I didn't feel like getting creamed right then.

We barely even drove out of the parking lot before the twins fell asleep.

"Oh sure," Maggie hissed, "*now* they fall asleep." She bit some skin off a finger. "We *are too* old enough to stay there. But who cares? It's only *my* birthday present, two weeks late."

I didn't say anything. I was still uncurling my toes.

Then Maggie's mom called from up front that since the twins were asleep she'd take us to the library. She'd wait in the car while the twins napped. "It won't take as long as the haircuts and the whole trip won't be a waste. Okay?" she said.

I said okay — it sounded pretty good to me. Maggie didn't say anything. That made me squirmy but her mom laughed "Okay" back, as if Maggie was doing cartwheels for joy.

The library was busy, too, but we didn't have to wait. I stopped to look at all the Hallowe'en books out by the bulletin board. Maggie went over to the adult section, where they had books under this sign that said HELP FOR HOME HANDYPEOPLE. After that I forgot about her, I was so busy finding books for Readathon. They had to be not too dumb — so I wouldn't get bored — and not too long — so I could finish them in time to put them on my list. When I spotted Maggie again, she was in a big hurry. *And* she wouldn't show me all her books. There was one she kept shuffling to the bottom of the pile.

When we got back to the van the twins were still snoozing. Maggie's mom was, too.

It wasn't until we were in Maggie's backyard, in the tent that our old teacher Mr. Flynn had given us, that she showed me the book. THE HOW-TO BOOK OF HOME HAIRCUTTING. On the cover was a picture of this kid with a checkered tablecloth around his neck, grinning like a nerdoid while his mom chopped his hair off. Maggie was grinning too — her I've-got-a-secret smile. She peeked out the tent flap, then closed it and said, "The Maple Avenue Marvel strikes again, Cyril. It's haircut time!"

The Alien Invaders alert went off in my brain. It always did when Maggie said stuff like that.

"No way," I said. "Anyway, your mom said we'd go back later." I wasn't sure I wanted to go back to Hair Today, but I was sure I didn't want a haircut from Maggie.

"Get real, Cyril. We'll never get back there. But

with this book we can get any haircut we want. And no waiting. Look, this shows the whole thing. It'll be easy. We'll surprise everybody." Maggie almost purred that last part. She liked surprising people.

It was starting to sound pretty decent, even to me. "Are you sure we can do it?" I asked.

Maggie waved the book. "*Easy.* You just have to do what I say. Could I get something this cinchy wrong?"

Maybe, I thought, but I said, "Welllll ... It's too cold in here."

"It is not, Cyril." Then Maggie gave me the evil eye. "C'mon, do you want to look good for Lucinda Peebles or not?"

I felt myself turning red all the way down to my socks. Nobody was supposed to know about Lucinda Peebles.

Like she was reading my mind, Maggie said, "Everybody knows, Cyril. You only make goo-goo eyes at her all day. Now she'll stare back at you. On Monday. Thanks to me."

I thought about Lucinda Peebles staring at me. It was like thinking about sports and chocolate cake at once. I wasn't going to say that to Maggie, though. I said, "Oh yeah, like you're helping me with — "

"I'm working on it, Cyril," she snapped. "Now is this a deal or not? Partners?"

I took a deep breath. "Partners," I said.

We snuck into Maggie's house and grabbed this little mirror and a comb from Maggie's dresser and a bunch of scissors because Maggie didn't know which were the sharpest. Maggie took a sheet from the laundry then wet my hair in the wash tub because I was getting the first cut. She used the cold tap. When I yelled she just about stuffed the sheet down my throat.

"Be quiet," she hissed. "Now, stick your toque on and let's get out of here." On the way out she swiped a lawn chair from the garage.

Back in the tent, Maggie opened the chair and I sat down. It wobbled.

"Sit *still*," she ordered, and wrapped the sheet around my neck.

"Gaaack!" I shouted. It was all I *could* shout, the stupid sheet was so tight. Maggie loosened it about one micromillimetre and made me stick my hands out so I could hold the book up for her. Then she started to work.

It was probably more fun than sticking dirty gym socks up your nose, and it probably didn't hurt more than getting hit with a steamroller, but I still didn't like it. The only sharp scissors were the little curved ones for toenails. The wet hairs started falling down the back of my neck and itching like crazy. Maggie kept twisting my head around and telling me to sit up straight. And she practically pulled my ears off with the comb. I'd be itching and trying not to move while she flipped the pages in the stupid book. It took forever, and my head was freezing.

Then Maggie was stopping for longer and longer. She'd grab the book out of my hands and stand behind me; then she'd snip like crazy for a minute —

first one side, then the other. Then she'd stop again. Every time I asked for the mirror she'd say to wait, she was too busy.

Finally, after a really long pause, she said in a strange voice, "I'm done." She came around in front of me. Her eyes were big and she was biting at her lip.

"Let's see," I said.

Maggie had the mirror in her back pocket. Before I could reach it, she'd ducked out of the tent. "I'll go wet my hair," she called. "Be right back!" Then she was running for the house.

I reached up and patted my hair — it only felt cold and wet. I jammed my toque back on and breathed out some more dragon clouds.

Maggie came running back with her head wrapped in a towel. "Where's the mirror?" I said.

"There's no time for that, Cyril." She plonked down on the chair. "Do my haircut first. It's freezing out here."

I could have told her that.

Maggie put on the sheet and held up the book in front of her. "Just do exactly what I say," she said, and read out loud about how to comb out her hair.

If Maggie cutting my hair wasn't as bad as old socks up the nose, cutting Maggie's hair was worse. Worse than sitting in cold spaghetti or falling in the toilet. Maggie yelled every time the comb pulled even the tiniest bit of a tangle, and I couldn't hold the hair right with my fingers. The nail scissors hurt my thumb, and they made all my cuts go in curves instead of straight lines. I was biting down so hard my tongue hurt, too.

Maggie snapped orders at me every five seconds, telling me to do stuff that you just couldn't do, until I got all sweaty. I kept saying okay and chopped a lot of hair off the back, where it was really long, just to be cutting something. That made the front too long, so I snipped it, too. The side parts looked weird then, so I started on them, but when I was done, they looked like something from outer space. In fact, everything looked weirder. The curve in the scissors had left all these little spikes of hair sticking out all over — except for this one place on top where I'd zoomed off a whole bunch because I couldn't get it to lie down. *There*, it was like her hair just shrivelled up and died.

I turned the scissors and tried to snip off some of the spikes, but all I did was make new ones. I combed for a minute and decided to even up the bottom edge all the way around instead. It ended up looking like the line you make when you draw waves. Now I was really sweating. I kicked at the pile of hair on the tent floor. A few fallen leaves were mixed in with it. Maggie was going to kill me.

I took a deep breath and said, "I'm done." I sounded like a strangled mouse.

"It's about time." Maggie jumped up and started brushing herself off. "How's it look?"

"Well," I said, "it's different than before."

"Let's go see," she said.

Half of me wanted to sneak away right then, but

the other half wanted to see my own haircut. I pried the scissors off my hand and followed Maggie across the backyard. From behind, her head looked like one of those round, spiky mines that blow up ships. My stomach went all soggy.

Maggie opened the van and we climbed in the front. I pulled off my toque. "Okay," Maggie ordered, "look at the same time. Ready? One, two, three, go!" She swung the mirror down.

Neither of us said anything for a long time. Finally, Maggie said, "Well, they don't look *that* bad."

"Nah," I lied, "they're okay." I had to make myself start breathing again.

"It's probably the way we have to bend to see in this little mirror," said Maggie.

"Right." We didn't look at each other as we climbed out of the van. My toque was pulled right down to my ears. Maybe I could wear it until spring. I took the long way home and then went into my backyard and walked around a couple of times. Fenways' hairy hamburger dog was in their backyard. It started yapping as soon as it saw me. I didn't care. I was just making the long way home longer.

It still wasn't long enough, though. When I finally went in the house, my mom said I couldn't wear my toque inside, and when I took it off, she practically shot up the chimney. That's when the telephone started humming between my house and Maggie's. About one minute later my dad and I were picking up Maggie in his old hatchback and heading back to the mall.

We came out of the Hair Today shop with heads like hard-boiled eggs. All my dad said was, "Well, kids, hair today, gone tomorrow." I felt like a total nerdoid. My toque was on before he even finished chuckling.

Maggie was grinning so hard I thought her teeth would crack.

"Have you seen how we *look*?" I moaned.

"Exactly, Cyril," she said.

"You *like* this?" I stared.

"Sure. It's what I wanted. Didn't you hear what the stylist said?"

I'd heard, and it didn't make any difference. The lady that cut our hair had a brush cut, too, and she said ours was going to be the most popular style in a couple of weeks. She'd already done five today.

"Well," I said, "at least in a couple of weeks there'll be lots of people looking like this."

"Yeah, too bad," Maggie said. "Oh well, maybe I'll win a contest by then. Which reminds me, Cyril." We were a step behind my dad. Maggie leaned in close so he wouldn't hear. "Don't forget to fill out those entry forms. If I won a good contest I wouldn't have to make complicated plans like this one."

"What one?" I grumped. "You made a dumb plan about giving haircuts and you blew it."

Maggie smiled her I'm-totally-brilliant smile. "Oh, no I didn't. I had to get us back here somehow, didn't I?"

"Get out," I said. "You planned this? *Get out!*"

"All I'm saying is maybe I wanted this haircut and the only way I'd get it was if I let you wreck my hair."

"You said it wasn't that bad," I hissed. "And why'd you have to wreck mine, too?"

Maggie looked surprised. "I thought you wanted a haircut. And Lucinda-poo's going to looooooove it, Cyril. She'll probably want to elope."

"Oh, shut up, Maggie," I said, but I got that sports-and-chocolate-cake feeling again for a second. My dad was getting way ahead. I hurried after him.

"Just relax, Cyril," Maggie whispered. "If we gave each other good haircuts, my plan worked; if we messed up, then we'd have to get *real* hairstyles. It was perfect." She took a last nibble on her little finger and waved her hands in the air.

It was, too. In fact, the more I thought about it, the more it sounded too perfect. "You didn't have this plan, you made it up after, to fit what happened," I said when we got back to my place.

"You can think whatever you want, Cyril. But remember, it's going to take a genius to help you with —"

"Not now!" My dad was still outside.

"Just don't forget those contest forms."

The longer I looked at her the less I knew what to think. Maybe she *had* planned it all. Maybe Lucinda Peebles *would* go gaga on Monday. But in the meantime ... I pulled my toque down nice and snug, then stuffed my hands in my pockets. The contest forms still felt as big as the telephone book.

"See you later," Maggie said over her shoulder, then started to run. The short way.

"Hey," I called after her, "Fenways' dog is in their back—" but by then it was too late. I could already hear the barking. Oh well, even Maggie couldn't always be right. Maybe that was why we were friends.

Chapter Two

"HEY, CYRIL, WHAT HAPPENED, RUN INTO a lawnmower?"

"Hallowe'en's *next* week, Chrome-dome!"

"Whooo, smoooooooooooth!"

Maggie was wrong about Monday morning. I couldn't find Lucinda so she could notice my haircut, but then after about two minutes in the school yard, I hardly cared.

"Hey, Cyril, who lowered your ears?"

"Forgot your wig, Bald One!"

By then I wanted to turn into a rock or something. I mean, rocks are bald, but nobody laughs at them.

Maggie didn't get teased, she got Russell Hummaker. Maggie and Russell had been at war from about one minute after Russell's family moved into Maggie's old house on Greenapple Street. Now Russell showed up with Maggie's same haircut. As soon as Maggie saw she wasn't going to look different from everybody, for even one day, her eyes got all narrow. And when Russell called her a copycat, she called him one back. Then Russell said no he wasn't because his head didn't look like a bowling ball and

Maggie said he was right, his head was only the size of a ping-pong ball, and then they really got going.

By the time we went into class I was wondering if my mom could knit me a toque long enough to roll all the way down to my shoes. I could hide in there for two weeks, until everybody looked bald. I was also pretty steamed at Maggie. I was getting teased and she didn't even notice, she was so busy being at war with stupid Russell. "Thanks for making me the big joke of the morning," I snapped.

"Cy-rilllll. Don't be so chicken. Listen, as soon as I finish off micro-brain Russell, I'll help you out. I'm going to tell him his hair is the only thing shorter than he is. He'll probably disintegrate."

"Oh, who cares." I rolled my eyes. I couldn't see any hair when I did it. That made me feel worse.

"Believe me, Cyril, it's important. Anyway, who cares what *they* say. All you care about is what *Lucinda* says." Maggie gave me a little kick on the shin.

"Maggie! *Shut up*, willya?" I didn't want the whole entire world in Room 9 to know. But Maggie was kicking me again. Lucinda had just walked in.

She was with Tanya and Karina and a bunch of other girls. I watched her red hair bobbing and the way her nose crinkled up into her freckles when she giggled. I got the sports-and-chocolate-cake feeling again, but with staying up late to watch TV added in, too. She hung up her coat and started to turn my way. I gulped down the boulder in my throat and held my breath.

"HEY RUSSELL! SCALP CITY OR WHAT?" Bobby Devlin yelled from across the room, and Lucinda's head whipped around the other way. Next thing I knew she was running over there, giggling that Russell was not scalped, it was a nice haircut. *What about mine*, I wanted to yell, but I felt too much like a flat tire to say anything. Besides, Maggie was dragging me over to the Readathon bulletin board.

More bad news. Everybody had a piece of paper on the board, where you wrote down the titles of the books you'd read. We both wrote down our books from the weekend, but Russell was all of a sudden leading everyone by three books.

"He probably only reads the first sentence."

"First word is more like it," Maggie said, then the bell rang and Old Lady Loony walked in.

Our teacher's real name was Mrs. Van Loon but nobody called her that — just Old Lady Loony or the Looner. At first nobody had even believed that she could be married, but my mom said that she was for sure. I figured the guy must look like Frankenstein but my mom said he was pretty normal. She'd met him when she and Old Lady Loony taught at the same school, back before I was born. My mom said the Looner was about fifty, so at least we were right about her being ancient.

She came sailing through the door that morning, then stopped dead and stared down her nose at Maggie. She had these little glasses, with the tops cut off, that she always gave you the x-ray eye over.

With her orange hair piled up and her glasses sliding down, her face looked about eight miles long.

Her bony old finger flicked out and all her bracelets jingled. "Maggie, where are your shoes?"

As soon as she said it, I checked my own feet. I knew I was wearing shoes, but she just had that kind of voice.

Maggie said, "I forgot them at home." It was a pretty soggy morning and a lot of kids had worn boots.

"Then it's down to the office after announcements. Ask Mrs. Singh for shoes from the lost and found. There'll be no stocking feet in Mrs. V's classroom. That's a rule you know very well."

Maggie turned fourteen different shades of purple. There was nothing worse than shoes from the lost and found. They made you think they'd been lost on purpose, they were so old and stinky. Our last year's teacher, Mr. Flynn, let us wear sock feet if we forgot, but not the Looner. Maggie bit at her thumb. Her eyes were all narrow again as we went back to our desks.

Old Lady Loony dumped her giant-size purse on top of the file cabinet, opened the drawer of her desk, and pulled out a pitch-pipe. Then she said, "Good morning, everybody," in the way that told you to answer, "Good morr-ning, Mrs. Van Loon," in your robot voice.

"All stand for the national anthem." She held the pitch-pipe with the tips of her fingers, like it was a chocolate cookie, and puckered up to sound the note. I always liked that part because it made her chin disappear into her neck. She looked like a prune with earrings.

We started off singing. We were pretty crummy. No matter how hard she glared, most of us just mouthed the words and the rest sang really quietly. The Looner sang so loud her neck skin wobbled. Bobby could do a great imitation of her singing: he gobbled like a turkey.

We sat down and, right off, four kids got nailed for not doing their geometry homework. When Maggie came back from the office, wearing one purple shoe and one checkerboard shoe, she made it five. Usually Maggie could answer homework questions in one second, even if she hadn't done the work, but that morning she got caught red-handed. After that, a whole bunch of us blew our answers. I even had one right, but the Looner got me so nervous that I wrecked it up.

"This, people, is not BETTER THAN YOUR BEST, and that is what we do in my class. What does this sign say? Russell!" The Looner smacked the blackboard with her shiny fold-up pointer. She was always swinging that pointer around.

"It says 'Think Big,' Mrs. V," Russell said, like the complete suck-up he was. His homework probably wasn't even done, either. He just didn't get caught, was all. He knew she liked being called Mrs. V, too.

"Well, congratulations, Russell. You're obviously one of the few people in this room who understands it." She glared a couple of laser beams out from behind her glasses; Maggie faked a yawn. Maybe that's why we all got extra homework.

But the worst part of the day was lunch. Lizards' gizzards, did I hate lunch. Just thinking about it made my stomach hurt worse than being hungry did. Maggie got to go home because her mom was there with the twins, but my mom was teaching and my dad worked at the newspaper — which is why I had this special problem.

See, nobody at our house liked to make lunches, so at the end of summer my mom got this idea. She bought about eight million loaves of bread and stuff, and one Sunday she made me and my dad help make enough sandwiches to last us all for about eighty years. We put this humungous pile of sandwiches in little plastic bags and stuck them in the freezer downstairs.

The stupid sandwiches froze okay; the problem was when they unfroze. The soggy, mushy ones looked the worst, but the sandwiches that were still frozen when you bit into them were the grossest ever. It was so bad that kids gathered around when I opened up my lunch, just to see how hugely pukey it was going to be. What made it totally unfair was Lucinda Peebles *always* wanted to trade lunches with everybody and I couldn't even show her what I had, in case she threw up.

I'd complained about it every night till my mom told me we weren't going to talk about it any more. She said she and my dad had to eat the same lunches and they weren't *that* bad. Besides, no way were we going to waste all those sandwiches.

That's when Maggie said she was going to help, but she never did. In the old days, Maggie liked problems, but now — it was different somehow. Oh, we still made deals and stuff, but she practically never did her half. I could fill out contest entry forms till doomsday, but when it was her turn to help me, she'd start making excuses and biting her fingernails. My mom said it was a wonder Maggie had any fingers left. I didn't care about her stupid fingers. I was more scared Maggie didn't want to be friends any more. My stomach would go all squashed when I thought about that. But the very next minute she'd get all excited and get me to do haircuts or something, and everything would be like always. I just didn't get it.

So there I was in the lunch room, mixed up about Maggie, starving, practically bald, getting teased, Lucinda Peebles twitching her nose and making her red hair swish around for everybody but me, and what do I find in my lunch bag but this yuckoid gunk that used to be a tuna sandwich. I whomped it right in the garbage and ate my apple. I was so mad I *felt* like starving. I wished it was the old days, with Mr. Flynn teaching and my dad at home writing and Maggie being the Maple Avenue Marvel.

At the end of the day things got a teeny bit better. Right before the bell, Old Lady Loony told us that we should all start thinking of ideas for our Hallowe'en party. She said we'd plan it on Friday. And then she handed out permission forms for a field trip to the East Field Study Centre. The trip was in November and it was going to be a sleep-over.

Frozen potatoes, did the place ever go nuts! You could barely hear the bell ring. The Looner yelled "QUIET!" even louder and looked at us as if we'd wiped our noses on the curtains or something.

"That will be just about enough." The words came out all chopped off. "That kind of behaviour won't earn you a party or a trip, so let me remind everyone that no one is going who isn't doing —" She raised her arms and eyebrows at the same time and we all chanted, "BETTER THAN YOUR BEST."

"Hear, hear," said the Looner. "And don't forget your HOMEWORK." She gave us a killer laser beam over the glasses and the day was done. I gave Lucinda one more chance to notice my hair, but she was listening to Monica, and Monica talked forever.

"Let's *go*, Cyril." Maggie was right behind me.

I picked up my books. Maggie didn't have any.

"No homework, Maggie?" The Looner's voice was so scary I fumbled my books.

As I bent to pick them up, Maggie said, "I'm done already."

Old Lady Loony lifted one eyebrow. "I hope you are."

Next morning, whammo, Maggie had to do the very first homework question. Maggie said, "Easy," and aced it. She did it every time, all day. That night she didn't take any books home again and still got perfect in spelling the next day. Thursday, the Looner called her over to her desk.

"What'd she say?" I wanted to know.

Maggie made her this-is-so-dumb face. "She said I was lucky school is so easy for me but she doesn't want me showing off; I might give kids like you bad habits. Why don't I behave like Russell and set a good example for everybody."

We just about popped a gut, laughing. Russell was all goody-goody when Old Lady Loony was watching, but he was always getting Bobby to make faces and stuff behind her back.

Then I stopped laughing.

"What'd she mean, kids like me?" That sounded like I was dumb or something.

"She called you a hard worker. She said, 'It would be a shame if hard workers like Cyril got the wrong idea from you.'" Maggie tried to make her voice go like Old Lady Loony's. It didn't sound much like her, but I didn't care. Questions were going off in my brain like popcorn. A hard worker. Did that mean she liked me? Did I want to be liked by Old Lady Loony? Would Maggie still like me if the Looner did?

I was getting the soggy-stomach feeling so I had to think fast.

"So like, if you're getting your homework done so fast, you've got lots of time to work on my lunch problem now, right?"

"I wish, Cyril. I've got to keep track of all my contests, and there's Readathon, and helping with the twins ... It's a good thing I *don't* have homework!" Maggie said the last part really loud, and *blog*, the soggy feeling got mixed with being mad.

I whispered, "You'd better watch out or Old Lady Loony will get you. She might not let you go on the trip or something," and a part of me was almost hoping it would happen.

"Oh, who cares if it bugs her, Cyril? How can she stop me if my marks are great?"

I snapped, "Maybe she thinks you can do better." Maggie didn't notice the way I said it.

She sniffed. "I don't have to." But she was munching a finger when she said it.

Next day was Friday, and I didn't have time to worry about Maggie because we planned the class Hallowe'en party. That's what the Looner said we were doing, anyway, but she shot down just about every good suggestion. Okay, some of them were just a joke, like when Bobby said we should play spin the bottle. I'd had to play it at a Valentine's party once and it gave me jelly knees. But when I saw Lucinda blushing like crazy, I was almost sorry the Looner said no.

I wasn't sorry for long. Russell stood up and said his mom thought we had too much candy at Hallowe'en. Why not just have stuff that was good for us at the party? Everybody groaned so hard the Looner had to say no. She gave Russell a totally sick-making smile, though.

Finally it got worked out: Lester could bring his tape player in and we could choose one tape each. Everybody had to wear a costume and bring three snacks, and there'd be lemonade. Then the Looner said we'd play charades and musical chairs. Everyone groaned again but she said she wouldn't have parties where everyone just stood around and acted silly.

That's when Maggie put up her hand and, in her friendliest voice, asked, "Why don't we have a haunted house?"

Everybody got excited.

"That's too much work, I think," said Mrs. Van Loon.

"I'll do it," Maggie said. "And maybe Cyril could help — after he gets his homework done."

What was going on? Yesterday Maggie didn't have any time and today she was talking like we were partners again.

Before I could even think straight, the Looner was saying, all interested, "Will you, Maggie?" She jangled the bracelets on her wrist. "Do you think you can manage to help, Cyril?"

"Uh, yeah, er, sure. I guess."

"Well done," said Old Lady Loony. "That's a very good idea, Maggie. I'll find a room we can use. Now then, get out your spelling workbooks and add these words to your lists. We'll check them Monday."

For a second I was too stunned to move. Maggie wanted my help and Old Lady Loony had told me, "Well done." As I shook my head to see if my ears were working right, Maggie leaned over and whispered, "Cyril, I've got a plan."

Chapter Three

"JUST LISTEN TO THIS, CYRIL, AND AFTERWARDS you can tell me how perfect it is." We were sitting in the den at my place on Saturday afternoon. The TV was on, not to watch — it was a nerdo bowling show — but so no one would hear what we were saying. They did that in a spy show we saw once. Outside it was pouring. The cars parked along Greenapple Street had brown leaves plastered all over them. The whole world looked as soggy as one of my sandwiches.

"Now pay attention, Cyril." Maggie pulled a book out from her backpack. "There's haunted-house instructions in this library book and I've got plans, too. It'll be excellent. And what will be even more excellent is that Old Lady Loony will love us for doing it, and it isn't even homework. In fact, we probably won't have to do any — " Maggie stopped to nibble on a finger while my mom went by the door. "We can just say we're too busy with this."

No homework would be great but something sounded fishy to me. "I thought you didn't care if the Looner liked you," I said. I didn't say I thought she already liked *me*. "And what about my lunches? You promised."

Maggie acted as if she didn't hear me. "*And* if we make it really scary, Cyril, Lucinda is going to turn all pale and blubbery and somebody strong and fearless will have to make her feel better by telling her it's all make-believe. She'll be a damsel in distress." Maggie fluttered her hands and eyelids as if she was going to faint. "With Lucinda it's more like a dumbsel in distress, but somebody will have to be her hero. Hmmmmmm?" Maggie whacked me in the ribs.

I hardly felt it. It was chocolate-cake-sports-up-late-watching-TV time again. I saw Lucinda fainting in my arms while all the other guys were shaking with fear, just like in the book about Robin Hood I'm reading for Readathon. In fact, that was who I'd go as on Hallowe'en! It was *perfect*. There she'd be, fainting. Then her eyelids would flutter and she'd gaze up at me with her blue eyes. Or were they green? I'd never been close enough to tell. Now I could find out.

"Partners?" asked Maggie. "No homework? Rescue the dumbsel?"

"*Damsel*," I said. "And we do my lunch problem right after."

"Yeahyeahyeah, suresure. Now, partners or what, Cyril?" Maggie bounced up and down on the couch.

"Partners," I said.

We made plans until my mom stuck her head in the door and asked Maggie how her mom and dad and the twins were. They talked for a little while, then Maggie got ready to go. As she was putting on her jacket, my mom said, "No boots and raincoat, Maggie?"

"She's taking the short way," I blabbed, before I even thought.

"The short way?" my mom asked. We'd never told our parents about it.

"Cyril means I'm running," Maggie said. She bent over to tie her shoes. "I go faster without boots and stuff. You stay drier that way. It's a scientific fact." She straightened up and rocked back and forth, looking around as if she'd never seen our house before.

"Hmm. And your mom doesn't mind you going out like that?" my mom said.

"No. Besides, she's busy with the twins today," Maggie said, reaching for the door. "They have ear infections."

"Well, hurry home. And tell her to give me a call if she needs a hand." Maggie bit a finger, waved goodbye and zoomed down the steps.

My mom closed the door. "Maggie's mom wouldn't send her out like that in this weather, busy or not. And it's not like Maggie to tell tales. Is anything bothering that girl, Cyril?"

"I dunno." I wasn't sure what to say, partly because I really didn't know much and partly because grown-ups can be tricky. You can't tell them *everything*. "She doesn't like Old Lady Loony much," I said. "Nobody does."

"Hmm." My mom sounded as if she barely heard me. "I don't think she sat still for more than five seconds all afternoon, and her fingers look so *sore*. She never used to bite them like that, did she?"

I shrugged.

"Well, something's bugging her," my mom said, and headed for the kitchen.

If she wanted to see someone who was bugged, I thought, she should see me any day at lunch-time.

* * *

By Hallowe'en we had everything done but our homework. Old Lady Loony nabbed us twice in two days. When Maggie said it was because of the haunted house, the Looner gave us her laser glare *and* extra work for that night, Hallowe'en or not. Maggie told me she could do the work in about two minutes and I could copy hers. That made me feel better, but everyone was still pretty scared by it. When Old Lady Loony got on the warpath, you never knew who'd get it next.

I didn't really start to feel good again until after lunch. My peanut butter sandwich was more like frozen mud on cardboard, but after lunch we got to put our costumes on and set up the haunted house in the boys' change room.

That's when it really started to feel like Hallowe'en. Decorations were all over the school — cardboard pumpkins and black cats and witches. Some of the teachers had costumes on, too. Mr. Huffer was a hobo with his cheeks all blacked like he hadn't shaved, and Miss Evans had on a clown suit with purple hair and funny make-up so you couldn't recognize her.

As we carried stuff past the office on our way to the gym, a gorilla suddenly swung through the doorway. I jumped so fast I almost dropped all the covered bowls of guts we were going to make people touch in the haunted house. The gorilla pulled off its head and it turned out to be Ms. McLean, the principal. She helped us carry stuff to the change room, to make up for scaring me. On the way, she asked what we were going to do. We told her some of it, but then she said to keep the rest secret, and she'd try to come see for herself.

When we got to the change room I got a chair and masking tape and stuck up strings of dental floss that Maggie's dad gave us. They hung right in the doorway and felt like spider webs when you walked through. Maggie put a table across from the door — that's where the guts bowls went, and right beside them she put this plastic skull her dad had from dental school. Then she took off for Room 9 and came back with the record player and this wicked sound-effects record we'd gotten from the library.

Next came the tricky parts. Maggie climbed onto the shelf that ran all the way around the room, reached way out, and taped the end piece from an old fishing rod to the ceiling, above the table. Tied to one end of the fishing line was this old glove that we'd stuffed with paper. We'd painted it green with red drips so it looked like a rotting, bleeding hand. Then we ran the line back to the shower stall in the corner. I was going to hide there, and when kids were touching the guts stuff on the table I'd lower the hand down behind them so it would be right in their faces when they turned around. Gruesome or what, eh?

And *then*, while they were still shaking in their boots, there'd be another surprise — heh, heh, heh. We'd put paper stuffing in some old clothes, to make a zombie. We stuck a knife in the front and smeared it all with red paint. It was only a butter knife because that's all my mom would let us have, but with just the handle sticking out it still looked pretty gory. Maggie had tied strings to the zombie's back. We kind of folded him face down in the opening of the shower and tossed the strings over the bar for the shower curtain. After I lowered the glove I would pull on the strings, and the zombie would stand up and raise its arms so you saw the knife and blood and everything. It was going to be grossly perfect, especially with the strobe light my dad had loaned us.

My dad said these strobe lights were really big at parties back when he was in high school. Anyway, this light had a black spinner that went around and around in front of it and made the light go flickery, so everything looked all jerky and broken up. I plugged the light in beside the record player.

"Okay, let's try it," Maggie said. "I go first."

I got in the shower and gathered up the thread and the strings. Maggie ran to the door and turned off the lights. It was incredibly dark. Then Maggie's flashlight came on and I heard her walking back to the table. The record player clicked and the flashlight went off. A terrible scream exploded in the blackness and I almost screamed myself. It was only the record player.

Suddenly the strobe light started up and Maggie yelled, "Hit it!"

Slowly I lowered the hand. Back in the shower, I couldn't see anything except for the flickering light. The record was making footstep and clanking chain noises now.

"Okay," Maggie called over the chains, "now do the zombie."

I jerked on the strings and the zombie started to move. A thunderstorm rumbled on the record. Suddenly Maggie was beside me, grinning. "You try it," she said.

I gave her the strings and everything and ducked out of the shower. From the middle of the change room, the record player sounded way louder. The light looked as if it was getting sliced up with knives. I lifted my hand. The light made it jump and dance like something from an old movie. On the record player, an owl hooted and an old door creaked open. I looked over to the table and saw the skull grinning at me. Was its jaw moving or was it just the lights? What was left of my hair prickled along the back of my neck. Then something else prickled back there, too.

I whipped around and found the green hand

hanging in my face. In the shattered-up light it looked alive. I jumped back. This terrified voice wailed "No, no, nooooooooo," and a diabolical laugh came out of the record player. That's when the zombie started to move. I nearly lost my lunch right there. I'd helped make the stupid thing and it still scared me.

No way was I telling Maggie, though. "It's good," I called as the record player went quiet for a few seconds. Then this incredibly loud train whistle came blasting out of it and *that* made me yell.

"Turn it off, Cyril," Maggie called, stepping out of the shower. "That's the end of the scary part." The change-room lights went on. I turned off the record and the strobe light.

"This is going to be great, huh?"

"Darn right," said Maggie. "That strobe light is fantastic."

"So is the skull," I said. We went on for a couple of minutes, saying how terrific each other's stuff was and how it'd be extra great if Ms. McLean came in. Lots of times Maggie was bossy as an army general, but after the crummy frozen sandwich and double homework from Old Lady Loony, this felt good.

"Didn't I tell you this would be better than homework?" Maggie laughed.

"Yeah," I said, and it was, way better. Except, I remembered, it had gotten us extra homework, instead of none. Maybe the Looner would forget the homework when she saw how much work we'd done. I sure hoped so.

Then the bell was ringing.

"Our costumes!" Maggie yelled, and we took off.

Room 9 was filled with witches, animals, super-heroes and all kinds of weird creatures. Even Old Lady Loony had this sparkly mask on a stick that she put up to her eyes sometimes. Bobby was a gangster. Monica was a fairy princess. Russell was an evil mutant space alien — Maggie said he was that every day anyway. Maggie was a gypsy fortune-teller. Lester and I were both pirates — I'd chickened out of being Robin Hood when my mom told me I'd have to wear green tights. Anyway, pirates had lots to do with fair damsels. I'd read a pirate book for Readathon, too.

Lucinda Peebles was over at Janice Myers' desk, dressed as a cat. Janice was a big orange crayon. She was in this tube thing with her legs and arms sticking out. At the top was orange cloth with a hole cut in it for her face, and a cone-shaped hat. It was neat and everything, but not exciting like robots or super-heroes.

I thought Lucinda had the greatest costume in the whole world though, all black with little cat ears and a tail. She had cat whiskers painted on her face, too, and she kept making them twitch by wrinkling up her nose. Every time she did it I added something to the chocolate-cake-sports-late-TV feeling: pizza, a million dollars, my favourite sweatshirt.

I tried to get over by Janice and Lucinda but I kept on bumping into stuff. My pirate eye-patch was mixing me up about how far away things were.

Never mind, I thought, Lucinda would get a good look at me when she woke up from fainting in my arms. I wondered if I'd have to kiss her.

But first there was a lot of other junk to do. There were charades and musical chairs, and then we just stood around and ate candy and chips until it was haunted-house time. After that, the Looner was going to read us a Hallowe'en story.

Maggie and I got to go down to the change room first. We could hear everyone giggling and talking outside as we checked everything one last time.

"Okay," Maggie said. "You hide in the shower. They come in two at a time. I make them feel the stuff and when you hear me say 'brains,' lower the hand, count to five and do the zombie. We'll scare their socks off. Just don't let anybody see you."

"What about when Lucinda faints?" I felt dumb as soon as I said it.

"Huh?" Maggie was busy with the guts.

"Nothing," I said, and clammed up, but Maggie had heard.

"Ohhhh, *thennnn*!" she said, with this disgusting smile. She put her hands over her heart and looked at the ceiling. "When the dumbsel faints, you leap from the shower like Robin Hood, so everyone will — "

"I'm a pirate. And it's *damsel.*"

"Okay, like Captain Hook or somebody," Maggie called as I turned towards the shower. "And if you *really* want to be a hero, you can show her the guts after. I put in some secret ingredients last night."

"Yeah, yeah, right. Just get started," I grumbled. I still had rubber legs from thinking about Lucinda and smooching, and the eye-patch had made me trip over the zombie and bump my nose. I was still rubbing it when the lights went out. Maggie said something out the door, then I heard her hurry back to the table. The door opened again and I heard Monica and Karina ask, "Do we come in?"

That's when Maggie started the record player and the strobe. The girls gave a little shriek, and then I heard them going "Ewwwww" when they felt the phony spider webs. Then I could hear Maggie making them feel all the guts stuff we'd done.

"Eyeballs," she said. "Skinned fingers. Lungs."

I could hear the gasps and giggles. "Brainnnnnns." I lowered the glove on its thread. "You can go now," Maggie said. That's when they screamed. I barely had the zombie halfway up before they were out of there. Perfect.

The next kids were already coming in the door. For the next little while I was so busy I could barely even breathe. Lower the hand. Raise the zombie. Lower the zombie. Raise the hand. Keep quiet. Don't trip over your pirate sword. Listen for the door. Listen for Maggie. Keep the eye-patch out of the way. And all the time the strobe was flashing away and kids were screaming and the record was getting louder. It was hard to tell who was coming in any more. How was I ever going to be able to rescue Lucinda if I didn't know it was her? Hot tomatoes, I wouldn't even know if *anybody* fainted out there.

The door opened again. There were boys' voices this time, Bobby for sure, and maybe Lester. They were really going nuts at first but they got quiet as they touched the pretend guts.

"Brains," Maggie said for about the millionth time, and I let the glove drop down. They yelled, and then I heard Bobby saying "What are you —" and Maggie shouted "Oh, no! Lester, you ca—" and then there was this kind of blubbery rasping and then the monster laugh from the record player. There was a smell like ketchup potato chips mixed with lemons and rotten eggs. Then Bobby was running for the door, yelling his head off, and Mrs. Van Loon was running in. I jumped and fell down, holding on to the zombie strings, which made this stuffed guy with a knife in his chest pop up right beside Mrs. Van Loon as the train whistle went off on the record, and she shrieked and went skidding through Lester's throw-up ... and that was the end of the haunted house.

Things were kind of jumbled up after that. We all went back to class, except Lester, who had to go lie down in the nurse's office. Old Lady Loony had to get another pair of shoes. We were hoping that she'd have to go to the lost and found, but she had her gym shoes in the closet. The Looner said we should have listened to Russell, there was too much junk food at Hallowe'en, among other things. She didn't say what the other things were, but she looked at me for a second and then at Maggie for longer. Everybody had to bring the stuff from the change room after the caretaker mopped up, and then we put all the desks in Room 9 straight. There wasn't time for a story after all.

While we worked, everyone talked about the haunted house. The kids that went through before it got shut down made it sound fantastic, but I didn't hear Old Lady Loony say it was so great. She was cleaning the bottoms of her pant legs, all red in the face from bending over, and glaring whenever she looked up. You could still smell the throw-up on them, no matter how hard she scrubbed. Ms. McLean had shown up too late to go through, just as the Looner was ordering us all back to class. I hadn't saved Lucinda Peebles, either.

Then, when Maggie and some of the others came back with the last of our haunted-house stuff, everyone saw it was just dumb old junk with paint on it. The kids who didn't get through, like Russell, started saying it couldn't have been that great.

"You'd better believe it was scary, Russell," Janice Myers argued, and a bunch of others said "Yeah, you better believe it." But then liar Bobby started saying that he hadn't really been that scared.

And that's when I got my big chance, because Lucinda Peebles hugged herself as if she was cold and said, "Well *I* would have been scared for *sure*. All those brains and everything. I'd have screamed." Her red hair swayed around her little black cat ears. I almost fell over, it was so beautiful. In fact, I did wham into a chair, but that was because of my eye-patch.

Before Russell could smart off, I practically shouted, "Well I can show you what it really was. Then it wouldn't be scary."

"Ewwwwww, no," gasped Lucinda. "Is it gross?" Her eyes got all big above her freckles. They were green — her eyes, I mean. Everybody else moved in close. They wanted to find out, too.

"Nah," I said. "It's not gross. It's funny." My voice sounded a little trembly and my face was getting hot. I mean, here I was, *talking to Lucinda Peebles*. My heart was whamming like a train engine. "I made it, so I know," I said, which was almost true. I'd helped anyway. Maggie had only finished it up and brought it to school. "Here, I'll show you."

I ran over to the counter by the sink and grabbed the margarine container that we used for the brains. On the way I did a quick practice pucker-up with my lips, just in case. My heart was whamming like *two* train engines.

Maggie grinned at me and whispered, "Don't forget, when you show the fair dumbsel, Cyril, there's secret — "

"Yeah, yeah, right," I said, and ran back to where they were all waiting. Maggie called after me but I was vrooming away too fast. I had to do it before I turned into mush in front of Lucinda. Mush was not romantic.

"Look," I smiled at Lucinda as if I did great tricks every day, "the brains were just cauliflower bits and mashed potatoes lumped together." Lucinda crinkled up her nose and gave a scaredy-cat shiver. Her hair swished. I pulled the lid off the dish.

That's when we screamed — Lucinda, me, everybody — and I dropped the container like it was a hot potato. Because whatever splattered onto the floor wasn't white and lumpy, it was gray and lumpy and streaked with globs of red and yellow. It looked exactly like ... brains. I swallowed something awful that came shooting up into my throat and took a step back.

That's when Old Lady Loony swooped in, took one look and snapped, "Who did this disgusting thing?" The room went dead. "I said, who did this disgusting thing?" Her bracelets jangled in the silence.

"I did," said Maggie, from over by the sink.

"Did you know about this?" The Looner glared at me. I shook my head. My voice had disappeared somewhere.

"And this filth is your idea of a joke, is it?" She whipped back around to Maggie. Her voice was shaking, she was so mad.

Maggie said, "It's only food colouring." Her face had gone white and she sounded all confused. I hadn't heard Maggie sound confused in a long, long time.

"Never mind what it's only, young lady. I've had just about enough of your humour for one day. I'll see you after school. Cyril, throw this sickness in the garbage right now, and the rest of you get back to work. Now, MARCH." She slapped her hand on a desk and I thought her eyes were going to burn the school down. Lucinda asked to go lie down in the nurse's office. Nobody else said a word until the bell rang. Then Old Lady Loony said not to forget our homework.

Everybody else left really fast, but I hung around my desk until Old Lady Loony told me to go. Maggie was sitting there staring straight ahead. I got my jacket and zipped it at the outside doors. Somehow, leaving felt almost as bad as getting in trouble. I mean, I was glad I wasn't in trouble but something didn't feel right. Maybe Maggie would be mad at me now.

I shifted my books around and stepped outside. It was hard carrying homework with a sword on. Everything was hard these days. I guessed we'd really blown it: homework on Hallowe'en, Lucinda sick, Old Lady Loony loonier than ever. Maggie and I weren't further ahead, we were a long way behind and never going to catch up. I put my eye-patch in my pocket and started up Greenapple Street, walking into the wind.

Chapter Four

MY PARENTS THOUGHT THE HAUNTED HOUSE was pretty funny, up to where Maggie got in trouble, anyway. I didn't tell them about the homework part or me screaming, or especially the Lucinda-falling-in-my-arms-plan part. At first I wasn't going to tell them anything at all, but it wasn't as if I got in heck and besides, they asked. I mean, it *was* my dad's strobe light. They got kind of mumbly when I said I didn't get it why the Looner was so mad. My mom said Maggie got carried away sometimes and Mrs. Van Loon was from a different generation. But so what? Grown-ups never want to cut up other grown-ups in front of kids.

Then my mom said, "Is this what you meant the other day when you said Maggie didn't like Mrs. Van Loon very much? Because she doesn't understand when Maggie gets carried away?"

"Not exactly," I said, and told them about the *better than your best* junk and how Maggie could ace everything, even if she didn't do her homework. I didn't say anything about *my* homework — which maybe was a big mistake because then my mom asked about eight million more questions about how Maggie was acting and what she said about stuff and did she get mad much.

Maggie, Maggie, Maggie. Blah, blah, blah. What about *me*, I felt like shouting. I was the one Maggie bossed around. I was the one who had to help her with all her dumb contests and who never got helped back, no matter how much she promised. I was the one who got nailed for double homework because of her. I was the one who had to squeal like a stupid baby in front of Lucinda Peebles. But I couldn't talk about that, could I? I put my elbow on the table and rested my head in my hand.

"Great manners, Cyril," my dad said. "Eat your dinner, please."

I said, "I'm not hungry," and I wasn't, any more.

"Well, if you hadn't eaten so much junk at school you would be."

"I had to," I said. "My lunch was so crummy I was practically starving to death. You should've seen how disgusting my sandwich was."

"Cyril, we're not arguing about lunches any more. You already know that." So I couldn't talk about *that*, either. Hot gizzards, if it hadn't been Hallowe'en the whole night would have been rotten.

When I went trick or treating that night I got nervous going up to Maggie's. What if they were angry about the haunted house? Maggie's dad was all cheery at the door though, even when I lifted up my eye-patch to let him know it was me. He gave me extra sugar-free gum.

Next day Maggie said she hadn't even told her parents she got in trouble because they wouldn't care. I didn't know what to think about that. She told me the Looner had gotten all squinty finger-pointy after I'd left Room 9 and told Maggie she'd better cut out the stunts and start acting as smart as she thought she was. "It's my way or the highway," she'd said. The Looner was going to give her one more chance to prove she should be allowed to go on the field trip. Maggie'd be a lot happier if she smartened up, Old Lady Loony said, and she wouldn't lead trusting friends like me into mischief.

What did *that* mean, I wondered. It sounded as if I was good, but it also made me sound dumb, as if Maggie could trick me into anything. It almost made me want to barge up to the Looner and tell her how wrong she was. Except, what if it got me in trouble?

At lunch that day the Looner called to me in the school yard.

"Cyril, I hope that in the future you'll stick to your work and not get involved in any more silliness."

I nodded. Looking right at the Looner scared me, so I looked at the monster purse instead.

"I know it isn't always your fault when other people lead you on, but I want you to get back to doing *better than your best*. Agreed?"

I could feel her photon disintegration beams on me. I said, "Yes, Ma'am," and kept nodding until she was gone. Then I took a big breath and went back to copying Maggie's homework.

After that I tried to forget the whole thing — I

had lots of other stuff to worry about, anyway. My lunches were still rotten, Lucinda wasn't in love with me, Readathon was on, and the Looner kept dumping work on us. The Hallowe'en pictures came down and all this nature study stuff went up. Everybody had an animal to look up, and every day we had to write down one geometric shape we found in nature. Gross potatoes, was it boring.

The only thing even halfway good was our field trip, and it was still over two weeks away. The best part for sure was going to be the sleep-over. Even Old Lady Loony couldn't wreck that. I got the tent from Maggie so I could set it up in the living room and sleep there, to practise, but my dad said there was the small matter of him and my mom using the room once in a while. My mom said the East Field Study Centre didn't have tents anyway, just a big room with mats on the floor. She'd taken her class to it last year. This year they were going to the West one, the same day we were going to ours. She said I'd need my sleeping bag though, so I got it out instead. It was great for pretending I was in a cave or at the North Pole, stuff like that.

But was Maggie excited? Did she even care? Did she think about all the stuff she said she'd help me with? Nooooooooo way. She just bragged about never having to do her homework. Once, when she didn't do the reading questions, she took my answers and gave them back with all my spelling mistakes fixed. Then she teased me for trying hard just so the Looner would like me. After that I sort of stayed away from her. She picked on other kids, too. Bobby called her the Queen of Mean and then a whole bunch of kids started calling her that. It all gave me a sour-milk kind of feeling. I'd had lots of fights with Maggie, and one time, just before she moved, we didn't talk to each other for nearly a week, but this felt worse.

The only thing Maggie was even halfway interested in was her contests and *I* was sick of them. I told her no more help until she helped me, but somehow, the Saturday afternoon before the field trip, she got me to come over to her place. Maggie's mom was going out and her dad was at his office, so we had to be babysitters.

The twins were snoozing when I got there, but not for long, boy. And disgusting gizzards, were they ever grumpy when they woke up, crying and drooling all over the place. Maggie said they were teething.

We couldn't get any contest forms filled out. That was okay with me, but it made Maggie a total crab-apple. She started slamming stuff around and bonked a glass of grape juice all over the carpet. That's when we smelled something, too.

I don't even want to talk about what it was like changing their diapers, except that Maggie's mom got home just as we finished. Right after she noticed the grape juice, she noticed Maggie hadn't plugged in the slow cooker, either. Her mom had reminded her at least seventy-five times before she left. Maggie said she hadn't remembered because the twins had been a world-record pain. Her mom said that lately Maggie was setting a world record for forgetting stuff. Maggie said she wished she *had* a world record because maybe then she wouldn't have to do dumb stuff like babysit.

I took off for home before things got even crabbier. I went the long way, even though Fenways' dog wasn't in their front window. They'd started putting it in the backyard, maybe because Maggie had taken the short way a whole bunch when we were planning the haunted house.

At supper my mom asked me about the afternoon and how Maggie did with the twins. She was pretending to be all I-don't-care about it, but her ears were practically elephant size, she was listening so hard. "She's not a happy kid right now, Cyril," she said at the end. "I hope her friends remember that."

Not happy? So, who *is* happy, I almost said. I was tired of hearing about Maggie. I mean, was Maggie unhappier than me? I took another bite of hamburger and thought about it. Maggie got to ride in their new jet-plane family van all the time; we had little cars. She was a genius who got perfect marks; I had to work like crazy. She always got to take the short cut. I had to take the long way. I got lunches so crummy that kids looked at them just to get grossed out. Lucinda never wiggled her nose at me. I practically got laughed out of the country about my haircut.

And did Maggie get teased? Noooo — well … She *was* at war with Russell and kids *were* calling her Queen of Mean. But she just crabbed right back at them. Did being crabby mean she was unhappy? I bit some more hamburger.

I knew Maggie was bugged about Old Lady Loony, and the Looner was pretty scary. She made *me* nervous, and she kind of *liked* me. But Maggie never sounded nervous. So why did my mom say Maggie was biting her fingers because she was nervous? My brain was getting tired thinking about it. Okay, Maggie was bugged about the twins, and she and her mom grumped at each other a lot. Would that make her nervous? She didn't grump at her dad though — he was always busy in the office.

I looked at *my* mom and dad. My dad had his mouth full and was trying not to snort too hard at something funny my mom was saying. We were having burgers and brown beans and salad, with chocolate glop for dessert. That slow cooker at Maggie's meant they were supposed to have stew or something yuckoid like that. I remembered the twins squawking and diapers stinking and Maggie and her mom complaining at each other, with the phone jangling away behind them.

Maybe Maggie *was* unhappier than me.

For a minute, I couldn't swallow. It was as if we were all of a sudden sitting on the ceiling or something.

Everything was still upside-down in my brain after supper so I went looking for my world record book. I guess Maggie arguing with her mom about world-record forgetting made me think of it.

Besides, I always liked reading the dumb ones, like piano smashing and eating raw eggs. But that night an idea started to prickle around in my head. If Maggie really was unhappy, I thought, and we were friends ...

It wasn't a genius-size idea or anything, but it was pretty good. And it wasn't because I was feeling all sad and mushy for Maggie, either. I mean, I was feeling a *little* bit that way, okay, but it was an idea for me, too. If it worked Lucinda would think I was a big hero, and my parents would be so excited they'd probably buy me pizza for lunch for the rest of my life. I started skim reading at hyperspeed.

The longer I read, the more I started to feel that maybe my idea was totally nutsoid. The record for bagpipe playing? Grave digging? I groaned. Then I read about the world's record house of cards. I stared for a long time, just to make sure it was really on the page. Then I ran for the telephone.

The line rang three times. Maggie answered. A twin was squawking in the background. I took a monster breath and said, like it was pretty boring, "Hey, want to get a world's record with me? I know one we can do."

* * *

The morning we left for the East Field Study Centre, Maggie was still yakking away about where we should make the pizza (that was our secret code for the house of cards), but when we saw all the boots and packs and sleeping bags in Room 9 and heard everybody talking and bustling around, even she forgot about it.

The Looner was peering through her cut-off glasses, checking stuff off on a clipboard. I'd figured she was born in school clothes, but there she was, in a purple sweater and stretchy green pants stuffed into red rubber boots. Monica's mom was coming along to help out. She was pinning name tags on kids' stuff. Bobby was trying to balance his lunch box on his head. Russell was holding a book in front of his face so everyone could see he was reading. He told anybody that even came near him that he wasn't letting field trips interfere with Readathon. Suck-up or what, eh?

We got on the bus right after announcements. I was trying to figure out how I could sit beside Lucinda and make it look as if it just happened, but I ended up squished between Maggie and Janice Myers. Bobby got to sit beside Lucinda. The Looner stood up by the driver. She'd put on a yellow kerchief and one of those big sweater jackets with crossed curling brooms knitted into it. Her monster purse looked like it weighed about three tons. She kept shifting it while she told us we were going to BEHAVE BETTER THAN OUR BEST, and I kept hoping it would bonk Russell in the head. As soon as she stopped talking he lifted his book up again so she could see he was reading.

"Maybe he'll get carsick," Janice Myers said. I hadn't known she didn't like Russell. Her face was pink. Maybe she was hot in her jacket.

Then the bus engine roared and everybody cheered. I laughed and looked out the window as we pulled away. Everything was zinging around inside as if it was my birthday or something. I tried to see my house as we rolled past Greenapple Street, but I missed it. Everything looked different when you were out of school and everyone else was in. The sky was gray. The radio had said bad weather was coming but that only made it better.

The bus roared again as it pulled away from the stop sign. We all went "Whooooah," and leaned as we went around the corner, and then we were bouncing along and everybody was talking over the roar at once.

"What if it snows?"

"Thirty feet of it!"

"Hey, what if we got stranded for weeks?"

"Say there was a hurricane ... but with snow!"

"No, a typhoon flood, and everything froze!"

"Know what? Then we could skate home!"

"Go by dog sled!"

"There could be a blackout!"

"Yeah, tell ghost stories!"

Pretty soon we were all saying how excellent it would be if there was a tornado blizzard, until the Looner yelled for us to PIPE DOWN. It was quiet for about two seconds. Russell held his book up higher and started making faces behind it. Maggie squinted out the window, chewing her lip. Then she whipped around to me and hissed, "You know what *else* a blackout would do, Cyril? No power? A little problem would be solved. Know what I mean?"

She was elbowing me like crazy. I leaned away and squashed Janice Myers. Her face was even pinker.

Maggie was still whispering. "Something would warm up, huh? Get it, Cyril?" She rubbed her stomach like she was drinking hot chocolate.

"Oh! Yeah, for sure," I said. I didn't have a clue — except for hot chocolate, and I knew that wasn't right — but I didn't feel like looking dumb.

"Exactly," said Maggie. "The Marvel strikes again." And then she didn't say another word.

The East Field Study Centre was in a conservation area. There was a forest and hills and fields and a lake that was gray like the sky. The bus let us off in a parking lot by some buildings. Across the way were wooden outhouses and a shut-up snack bar with rows of picnic tables tipped onto their sides, for winter. It made you feel summer was a long way away.

It was freezing cold, too. We took all our stuff inside the big building, where we were going to eat and sleep, then right off they took us on a nature hike. We got shown all kinds of stuff about the forest getting ready for the winter, but what we mainly saw was rain and mud. After that it felt great to go inside for lunch, even if mine was going to be icy baloney.

The room was about as big as our school gym and it even looked like it, sort of: there were basketball hoops at each end, and the same kind of tables and chairs we used for lunch-time. But underneath one hoop was a sliding shutter that opened up to show you the kitchen, and underneath the other hoop was a fireplace. The washrooms were down at the kitchen end, except one of them was broken. One of the Centre teachers told us that there were too many of us for one washroom; we'd also have to use the outhouses by the parking lot. Everybody went "Ewww!" and Bobby held his nose.

I ate with Lester and George and Janice and Karina, and for the first time all year, I almost made a lunch trade. I just about croaked on the spot when Janice asked me if I wanted to trade. The problem was she had egg salad, which is probably the only thing I hate more than frozen baloney. I figured she must've hated it, too, if she wanted to trade with me.

When we were finished eating they made us go back outside to play in the freezing cold until it was time for afternoon activities, whatever they were. A bunch of us ended up in the big field behind the building, playing army tag. More kids were over by the edge of the trees. A few others were down at the outhouses. A couple kids got soakers stomping puddles in the parking lot. Old Lady Loony sent them inside. You could hear her voice all the way across the field.

I didn't know where Maggie was until the trouble started. Monica was chasing me when we heard yelling and then Old Lady Loony's foghorn voice. By the time we all got near the outhouses, Old Lady

Loony was marching Maggie inside the big building.

Lucinda was bobbing and flapping her hands as if she'd grabbed a hot potato, blabbing away at intergalactic speed.

"Well, there was me and Bobby and Tanya and Russell, and we were right in front of an outhouse, okay, and then like Maggie's going by, okay, and Russell calls to her not to come too close or she might get locked in the outhouse, ri-ight? So Maggie goes 'Don't be stupid, Russell, the door only locks from the inside.' 'Cause you shut it with this little hook in there, ri-ight?" Lucinda always made her last word go all high and stretchy, like she was asking a question. She acted out all the parts, too.

"So then Russell goes 'Well you're so dumb you probably couldn't even lock it anyway,' and Maggie goes 'I'd rather be dumb than short,' and Russell goes 'Ha, ha, *I* could prob'ly even lock it from out here,' and Maggie goes, like, 'No way.' So they had this con-test? And the door got locked? And then like there was nobody insi-ide? So they couldn't get it open agai-ain? And they started yelling at each other, so then Old Lady Loony comes over and goes 'Who locked this door?' and nobody an-swers? So she goes all rang-ee and yells 'I said, who locked this door!' ri-ight? And Russell goes 'Maggie bet me she could lock the door from the outside,' and Old Lady Loony goes 'Maggie, did you lock this door?' and Maggie goes 'No,' okay, and then Old Lady Loony completely takes a hairy and starts yelling at Maggie, 'Don't you lie to me, young lady, I've had just about enough of this mischief and getting others into trouble. Don't you lie to me,' and she took her away." Lucinda was out of breath when she finished acting it out. All she could do was bug out her eyes and flap her hands one more time.

Everybody started talking and drifted away. I was the only one who stuck around long enough to ask how the door really got locked. Lucinda said, "With a stick. Bobby boosted Russell up and he slid it over the top of the door, so it fell down, right, and banged the hook."

"You mean Russell locked the door?"

Lucinda looked confused. She flapped her hot-potato hands again. "Okay, like Maggie said *she* was going to do it, but nobody would give her a boost."

I waited, but Lucinda only looked more confused. "So what happened then?" I asked. "Did she lock the door?"

Lucinda shrugged with her whole body. "We-lll, she was trying to. She went to drag a picnic table over? To stand on, ri-ight? And she had a long stick and everything."

"Yeah, but did she lock the door?" Was Lucinda really this dumb?

"Well, no, but yeah, like not exactly. Okay, while she was trying to pull over the table, Russell got Bobby to help him, okay, and he did it. But it was Maggie's idea and everything, okay, and she was *going* to do it."

"But she didn't. Russell did."

Now Lucinda rolled her eyes as if *I* was dumb.

Her face was almost as red as her hair. "Who cares? It doesn't matter, Cyril, if I said she was *going* to. And was Maggie ever mad. You should've seen the look on her face when she saw them. It was hilarious." Lucinda did her wrinkled-up nose giggle and swayed so the red hair bobbed below her tam. For the first time ever it didn't look that beautiful, but they were calling us for the first activity circle so I didn't have time to think about it. But I had a something-bad feeling that made a bigger cannonball in my stomach than the icy baloney had.

By the time somebody heard Maggie was going to get sent home, just about everybody had whispered it around that it wasn't Maggie who locked the door. Russell had even blabbed it himself a little, he thought it was such a good trick. Nobody said anything to the Looner, though, not even me. Partly, I guess nobody wanted to rat, even on a rat like Russell. I mean, some kids even liked him, or at least they didn't like Maggie. Bobby was going around saying "The Queen of Mean got beaned!" And us kids who did like her, I guess we all just figured that somehow Old Lady Loony would hear what really happened. Besides, Lester said, it didn't bug Maggie when the Looner got mad. She always said so. But every time I told myself that, I got this picture in my mind of the twins bawling and Maggie arguing with her mom and biting on her fingers. Something wasn't right. The cannon-ball started rolling in my stomach again.

In the end, Maggie didn't go home. The storm

hit first. It was hailstones mainly, then wind and rain blasting like you wouldn't believe. The power went off and the phone was out of order. Nobody could get in or out. It was great — scary, too. They had a transistor radio there and we heard that most of the city was blacked out.

So Maggie sat over against the wall, where the Looner put her, because she wasn't allowed to join in. She never said a word. We weren't allowed to talk to her. I couldn't even get her to look at me, and every time I turned around from looking, my stomach would go all lumpy again.

But late that night — late, late that night — after dinner and the sing-along and the fire in the fireplace and the stories and the hot chocolate and the whispering after they turned the lanterns out, way after everyone had gone to sleep, even, something woke me up. The storm had blown away and the night was still. I listened hard. The sound came back. It was crying. My cannon-ball started falling inside. It kept on falling for a long, long time. After a while the crying stopped, but the cannon-ball stayed in me till I went back to sleep.

In the morning all of Old Lady Loony's clothes were lying outside, soaking in the mud.

Chapter Five

THE POWER WAS STILL OFF ON GREENAPPLE Street when I got home. My mom and dad were at work, so I let myself in and dumped my stuff in the hall. Then I just listened to the quiet. It felt good after all the yelling at school.

After a while I kicked off my boots and went to the kitchen. I felt like I'd turned into a toad or something, that's how rotten I felt. The fridge was dark inside and for a second I didn't know why. Then I felt rotten *and* dumb. I grabbed some juice and cookies and went into the den. The TV wasn't working but I flopped on the couch anyway. Part of me was screaming to make a plan, but the rest of me knew that no plan was going to help now. Not one that *I* thought of, anyway.

Everything had gone wrong, first for Maggie and then for me. Maggie had gotten caught for wrecking Old Lady Loony's clothes about one second after we found them in the puddles. Even the red rubber boots were all pukey with mud. Maggie said she didn't do it, but there were tracks on the floor right to her sleeping bag, and there was mud inside it, too, from the leg of her sweat pants.

The place went nuts. Nobody knew what to say first: that it was a great trick on Old Lady Loony, or that Maggie was going to get killed now for sure. All at once it was like *anything* could happen and I didn't like it. It was as if there was something heavy stuck in my chest that I couldn't swallow down.

Hot gizzards, Old Lady Loony was scary that morning. Her face was all white and puffy, and there were zillions of tiny wrinkles around her mouth, like an accordion. Her hands were trembly and her lips kept working away as if she was chewing nails or something.

On the bus, Maggie had to sit by herself at the front. She didn't say anything and she never looked at me. She never even looked out the window. But every time I looked at her I remembered the crying in the night and my insides would scrunch up. When the bus stopped she got sent right to the office.

By the time we got back we'd spent the whole day whispering about how gross the mud was, and how George saw Old Lady Loony's pink underwear, and how they put her clothes in a big garbage bag, and did you see the Looner's face when her turkey neck got all wobbly, and maybe she'd have a heart attack, and how would we know if she did? Monica heard Maggie was going to get expelled. Patti said she'd only get suspended. Lester said she'd get the strap. Karina said her big brother had told her that a way long time ago, this boy had hung a dead chicken from the mirror in the Looner's car, and he went to reform school and ended up murdering a whole bunch of people. It was kind of sick, but interesting, too.

Then we told the whole rest of the school what had happened, everybody talking at once. I quit after a little while though because all they were blabbing about was pink underwear and dead chickens. Nobody was saying that Maggie never should have got in trouble in the first place because she didn't lock that outhouse door.

Maybe Maggie did wreck the Looner's clothes, but she did it because the Looner was wrong first. Only, it wasn't the Looner who was going to get murdalized. The more I thought, the wronger it seemed. And then *bam*, I had an idea. Not a whole genius plan, but a start: I'd get Lucinda to tell Old Lady Loony who really locked the outhouse door, because she told me and she saw it happen.

Everybody was standing in the hall outside Room 9, getting ready to go home, when I asked her. Lucinda was giggling about something, which made her freckles look *really* cute. For a second I went all chicken-livered, but then I blabbed out what I wanted.

Lucinda stopped giggling and looked at me as if I was talking Martian.

"She's not in trouble for the outhouse door now, Cyril."

"Yes she is. That started it. You don't have to say

who really did it, just that Maggie didn't."

"She did too."

My ears just about fell off. I said, "She did not! You *told* me. Russell did it and everyone knows."

"Well if everyone knows, then I don't have to tell." Lucinda shook her red hair back. "It was her idea anyway, okay? And she was going to. Russell was just quicker, is all. It's the same thing."

I stared at her as if *her* ears were going to fall off. "IT IS NOT THE SAME THING," I yelled. "If she'd have done it she would have said so, and Old Lady Loony wouldn't have got her into trouble for lying."

"IT IS TOO THE SAME THING!" Lucinda yelled back. "She lied this morning, didn't she? She lies all the time. And anyway, I hate her, okay? She's the Queen of Mean and she's always cutting up Bobby and Russell and me 'cause she thinks she's so smart. But she's *dumb*. You just want to get Bobby and Russell in trouble 'cause you're friends with her."

"SHE DOES NOT LIE ALL THE TIME AND SHE IS NOT DUMB. BOBBY AND RUSSELL ARE. AND YOU HAVE TO TELL!" I was jumping up and down like a kangaroo.

"Make me, Cyril," Lucinda spat.

"I don't make monkeys."

"Takes one to make one, nerdo. Get lost." She stomped away like she owned the world.

I was so mad, steam jets almost came out my nostrils. I'd tell Old Lady Loony myself. She probably thought Lucinda was just a nitbrain anyway: me, she'd believe. She sort of even liked me. All at once I could see it, how she'd thank me and apologize to Maggie and tell the whole class, and Maggie'd be so happy that she'd owe me forever and have to help me with stuff whenever I wanted, for about thirty years, but I'd never ask her because I was so nice. It was perfect!

"Where's Old Lady Loony?"

"She went to the office," somebody said.

"What are you going to do, Cyril?" Janice Myers asked.

"Just wait and see," I said, like some big hero. I fisted up my hands, made my eyes all squinty, and headed for the office.

Old Lady Loony wasn't there. Mrs. Singh said to try the staff room. I zoomed along the next hall, head down, and looked up about one microsecond before I'd have bashed into the Looner. She was standing at the staff room door, talking with Ms. McLean. I stopped like I had hypersonic brakes, teetering on my toes with my nose almost boinking her back. She was still in the purple sweatsuit she'd had for pyjamas and these dumb bunny slippers one of the teachers at the Centre had loaned her. She looked as saggy as the monster purse. Even her orange hair looked tired.

I took a big breath and said, "Mrs. Van Loon?" in my please-pass-the-butter voice. She didn't hear me.

I went up on my toes. "Mrs. Van Loo-oon?" I barely stopped myself from tugging at her like a little kid.

"Just a moment, please." She went on talking without even turning around. The Looner hated like anything to be interrupted, but there was no more time. My heart was whomping, the hall was crowded, all the words were ready to come out.

"*Mrs. Van Loon*?"

"*What* is it?" She whipped around, glaring. And whammo, total mush city. Cold tomatoes, was I ever scared. It was as if a plug got pulled out of my belly button and all the hero stuff went into a puddle at my feet.

I opened my mouth and blurped everything out as fast as I could. "Maggie didn't do the outhouse door, so she wasn't lying when she said it — somebody else did it but I can't say who it was but it wasn't her for sure because everybody knows she didn't they're just scared to say, and she does try she just pretends she doesn't because she's going to win Readathon isn't she, so she must try it's just that she's all busy because we're going to get a world record making a house of cards and she didn't lie for sure. She didn't."

Ms. McLean looked really hard at me while I was talking. She didn't look mad, but lizards' gizzards, the Looner sure did. Her eyes were zapping me and her mouth started to work, and I got scareder than I'd ever been in my whole life, just about. I looked at the floor.

The Looner breathed out a big sigh. It sounded like there were icicles dripping from it. "Thank you very much, Cyril. I'm sure you both mean well but this is none of your affair. It's time for the two of you to go home."

For a second I thought she meant Maggie and me, that it was all over. Then I saw Janice Myers standing beside me and it all crashed down again. Ms. McLean didn't say anything. Janice Myers' face was all red. I swallowed and said, "But —"

"I said, thank you."

I looked down. The bunny slippers turned back to Ms. McLean again.

I didn't look up again until I'd gone all the way down the hall. Janice Myers was gone, but I really didn't care because just then I spotted Maggie's mom coming in the front door. She didn't look any happier than the Looner. I whipped around and stared at all the old class pictures up on the wall until she was past. Then I took off for home.

* * *

And now I was all out of plans and everything was wrecked. Plus, I was freezing. I stuffed my feet under a sofa cushion to get them warm. I felt as if I'd been in the mud puddle all night with Old Lady Loony's clothes.

I wanted to *do* something. I jiggled the light switch. I wanted to *make* it work. Lights were supposed to work. Grown-ups were supposed to be smart. Frozen old tomatoes, if they couldn't even tell when you were telling the truth ... I mean, if grown-ups didn't know what was going on, who did?

Somebody had to. Because if they didn't ... I jiggled the light switch harder. I felt like kicking it.

I knew Maggie had to be fibbing about not wrecking Old Lady Loony's clothes. There'd been lots of times when Maggie didn't tell everything, but she'd never fibbed before. And if she was going to lie, why tell such a dumb one? It was even stupider than wrecking the Looner's clothes.

I still didn't have a plan when my parents got home. My dad brought pizza for dinner so I started to feel not quite so crummy. The lights came back on halfway through and we blew out the candles. My mom said she was glad we hadn't grocery shopped yet, because the food would have spoiled. *I* was glad we hadn't shopped *every* time we had pizza for dinner.

Then my dad told about what it was like at home during the storm, and my mom told about how it scared some of the kids on her field trip. Then I told about Maggie and the Looner. Most of it, anyway.

But telling it just made me feel crummy again. When I stopped, my dad cut some more pizza. "Well, it may be hard for Maggie not to be the centre of the universe any more, now that she has a baby brother and sister," he said, "and Mrs. Van Loon may not be her fairy godmother, but Maggie needs to learn that she can't always be the boss."

"But Old Lady Loony isn't fair," I said.

My dad snorted. "*Life* isn't fair, Cyril. But that doesn't mean you go around chucking people's clothes in the mud. Is Mrs. Van Loon fair to you?"

"I guess." I didn't want to say she liked me. And I wasn't going to tell how I got her mad at me that afternoon, either.

My dad nodded. "Then there you go. It takes two to tango, Cyril."

Tango? Before I could ask about that part, my mom said, "The trouble is, Mrs. Van Loon means well, but —"

"Means well?" Now I was snorting. My mom was talking teacher. I should have known. Teachers always stick up for each other when kids cut them up.

"Yes, she does mean well," my mom repeated. She didn't like being interrupted any more than the Looner did. "She wants you to do better than your best so you'll know you can, so you'll be able to do it for yourself later on."

I groaned. Yup, it was teacher talk all right. I made my lemons-with-broccoli face.

"Unfortunately, she's set in her ways and those ways may not be the best ones any more. But remember, Cyril, she's been at it for a long time."

Yeah, I thought, like since before dinosaurs. I went all saggy, like my bones had melted. My mom pretended she didn't see.

"And let's face it, huh, Cyril? Maggie can be … difficult. You of all people should know that."

"Remember your haircut?" my dad put in.

I wiggled in my chair and said, "But the Looner's out to get —"

"I don't think Mrs. Van Loon is out to get anybody." Now my mom was interrupting me. "Besides, Ms. McLean is a good principal and there are ways of handling these things."

"Yeah," I said, "like get rid of Old Lady Loony."

My mom shook her head. "If they can't get along, Maggie might end up in another class, but that wouldn't be good. It's like your dad says: there're times when you can't up and walk away from a problem, and Maggie might as well learn about that now. She'll have to learn to get along."

"Yeah, so," I said, "why doesn't Old Lady Loony learn then? Why does it have to be Maggie? Just 'cause she's not a grown-up."

"Because Mrs. Van Loon is the boss," my dad said.

"No," my mom said. "No, no, no." She sounded bugged with my dad now, too. "They *both* have to try to get along. Remember, I said Mrs. Van Loon is set in her ways? Well, so is Maggie. Just think about it, both of you. Maggie and Mrs. Van Loon are a lot alike. They're both stubborn, they're both smart, they're both used to getting their own way and they both — *bug* people till they get it. They're the same! I only wish I knew whether that's good or bad."

After dinner I went up to my room and peered out the window, over the backyards to Maggie's. I stood there in the dark and watched. The street light was shining in front of her house. Maggie and the Looner alike? Maggie changing classes? Even my mom and dad argued about it. Everything was still mushed up. Talking hadn't helped at all.

I thought about calling Maggie, but her parents didn't let her use the phone when they were mad at her. Then I wondered about sticking a sign in my window, in case she looked over, but I didn't know what to write and I didn't have any sign stuff anyway.

I switched on my lamp and opened my library book about King Arthur. I was still at the beginning part, where he's a kid and he pulls the sword out of the stone and Merlin knows he's going to be king. I flipped the pages, looking for pictures, and wished something like that would happen to me. Then I wouldn't need a plan. I'd just give orders, *zap*, *zap*, *zap*, and everyone would listen and do what I said. But there weren't any stones on Greenapple Street, not big ones anyway. Maybe I'd find a sword stuck in the Looner's desk. Russell would try. Maggie would try. Everybody would try. And then I'd go last of all. I'd jump up on the desk and with one hand I'd —

The telephone rang. I listened, in case it was about me.

"Hiiiiii, Pat," I heard my mom say. I knew it had to be Maggie's mom. I got off my bed super quietly and tiptoed along to the top of the stairs. It was no good. All I heard was my mom saying, "Yes, he did … Mm-hmm … mm-hmm. Well, I'll try," and then a whole bunch more "mm-hmms." All the juicy stuff was coming from the other end.

I'd never hear, unless — I knew what Maggie would do; I'd even seen her do it. I snuck back along the hall to my parents' room. Nobody was around.

So I did it, too, just this once. I yelled, "Hey, Mom?" and as she called back "I'm on the phone, Cyril!" I grabbed up the receiver so she didn't hear the click. I pressed my hand over the talking end. "Okay," I yelled. Then I held my breath and lifted the receiver up to my ear. Tricky or what, eh? Sometimes it paid to hang around with Maggie.

"Sorry," my mom was saying. "Anyway, you went to the school —"

Maggie's mom said, "Right. And of course I talked to Maggie and she was terribly upset, and I talked with the teacher and with Cathy McLean — after today I'm glad she's principal there, I'll tell you. She had something interesting to say about Cyril, too, that I think you'll —"

About me! My stomach took an elevator ride — down. I leaned in closer.

"Cyril!"

I jumped.

My dad was calling me from downstairs.

"I'll be down in a minute. I'm just finishing my page!" I got the receiver back up to my ear so fast I bonked my head.

Maggie's mom was saying, "... business about her lying and I just leapt in with both feet and said, 'My daughter does not lie. If Maggie told you she didn't do those things then she didn't.' And lo and behold Maggie does a complete about-face and says she *did* lie about the clothes — which of course makes me look foolish, and when we ask her why, she says because when she told the truth nobody believed her, so why should she bother. 'Nobody listens to me any more, anyway,' she said. I just felt so bad for her, Jan. And then this Mrs. Van Loon pipes up with —"

"*Cyril!*" My dad again.

I made another face. "Coming!" I was starting to sweat from keeping so still.

"... so I said to her that Maggie's marks didn't indicate any lack of effort, and she said that it was only a matter of time, that she'd seen it all before. So I said that maybe it showed something about her teaching —"

"Cyril! NOW!"

"In a sec," I just about screamed, "I'm, um, uh ... finishing some, some homework!" Bald potatoes, just when it was getting good. I whipped the phone back up.

"... McLean just guided things back on track beautifully, but all the time I just felt so terrible, felt it was partly my fault. You know, other years I've been *involved* with Maggie at school. This year, with the twins and the move — we just thought Maggie was coping. I don't know how we could have missed it."

Yeah, yeah, yeah, I thought. *Hurry up and get to the good stuff*. I didn't have much more time.

"Still, Maggie's going to apologize, and of course we're paying to have the clothes cleaned, but that doesn't solve the problem. Now Cathy McLean suggested some possibilities, and I wanted to find out what you think of them, as a teacher."

Finally. I was going to find out what would happen to Maggie. I just about stuffed the phone right into my head. "I'd also like your opinion of this Van Loon woman."

This Van Loon woman. Excellent. The phone was practically coming out my other ear. Suddenly I could see why Maggie liked listening in on her parents so much. My dad called again. I didn't even try to answer.

Maggie's mom said, "And one more thing: has Cyril mentioned anything about a bag of *brains* at Hallowe'en? Or about a world record in stacking cards?"

"A record for wha—?" My mom started to laugh. Something blooped inside me. Now Maggie was going to know I'd been blabbing. I almost groaned right into the phone.

That's when I heard my dad coming up the stairs. I froze. If I hung up the phone my mom would hear me. If I didn't, my dad would catch me. So I did something that I never want to have to do again. I crashed the phone onto the floor, leaped across the bed to the window and yelled, "Look at that!"

My dad zoomed up the stairs about twelve at a time. "Look at what? Hey, c'mon, Cyril, you've knocked the phone onto the floor and your mother's using it." He hung up the receiver and put the phone back on the bedside table. "Now, look at what?"

"Never mind," I said. "You missed it. I thought I saw a UFO but maybe it was just the street light."

"Uh-huh," my dad said. "I think you're losing it, Cyril. That's the kind of thing I'd expect from Maggie. Now let's get a move on. There's a sleeping bag and a pile of junk in the front hall. I can hear their little voices calling you to put them away."

By the time we got to the bottom of the stairs my heart had stopped thumping. My dad was right about one thing: it *was* Maggie's trick. She'd used it when she was trying to find out if she was going to get a baby sister or a brother. She'd never thought of twins.

I listened as hard as I could while I put my stuff away, but my mom's voice was too low all the time she was on the phone. It didn't get loud again until she'd hung up and headed down to the basement. Then she was yelling.

But that was about something else.

Chapter Six

ROOM 9 WAS CRAZY THE NEXT MORNING. Everybody was gabbing away at once: Maggie got expelled, Old Lady Loony had a nervous breakdown. Her husband was a cop and was going to arrest Maggie, Russell was after Maggie for telling on him, Maggie was going to get Russell.

I mostly kept my mouth shut. I didn't want to tell anybody what I'd heard on the phone 'cause they'd ask how I knew, and if Maggie ever found out I'd blabbed, she might cream me. The other news I had was only for her, so I just kept on listening and waiting for her to show up.

When the bell rang, somebody yelled, "She's coming!" We all shut up and Maggie and the Looner walked in — as if nothing had happened. Maggie had her queen-of-the-world look on. She stopped to check the Readathon board. The Looner had her make-up back on and her orange hair puffed up again. As soon as announcements were over, Maggie pushed in her chair and walked out of the room. Old Lady Loony told the rest of us it was time for geometry. And that was it: no news, no yelling, not even any whispering. It was terrible.

At recess I was a library helper, so I figured I wouldn't hear anything then, either. But when I walked in the library, there was Maggie with Mr. Huffer, the librarian. *All right*, I thought, but when Mr. Huffer went for coffee, I all of a sudden didn't know what to say to Maggie except, "Hi." My voice squeaked a little.

"Hi, Cyril." It sounded like the usual Maggie.

"Where did you go this morning?"

"Down here. From now on I get to come to the library two times a week for special lessons." She grinned but tried not to show it.

I squinched my nose up to make my *huuuh*? face. Maggie sighed but couldn't stop smiling. "Cy-rillllll. You get special lessons if you're special, right? And I *am* the Maple Avenue Marvel."

"Yeah, yeah," I said. "But what about Old Lady Loony and everything?"

"Oh, thaaaaat." Maggie made it sound like a thousand years ago. She shrugged. "Well, I had to say sorry about the clothes, and now I get special lessons. That's it."

"*That's it*! But what — I heard —" I stopped myself fast. I wasn't sure I wanted Maggie knowing I'd listened in to her mom.

Maggie said, "Ms. McLean knew I hadn't lied about the outhouse door. She knew all kinds of stuff, which made me pretty suspicious. Maybe she wears disguises: remember that gorilla suit? Or she listens on the PA ..." Maggie sounded as if she wished she could do that. "Or maybe she has spies, huh?"

I pretended to read book titles and hoped I didn't look like a radish.

"Anyway, so now I get to come down here two mornings a week. And, there's something else but I'm not supposed to tell." She leaned in close and told me anyway. "If everything isn't okay by Christmas time, I'll get moved to another class."

"Hot tomato gizzards," I breathed. Hearing it from Maggie made it real all of a sudden. The Looner's class was bad enough, but without Maggie it would be worse than eating fungus sandwiches.

Maggie shrugged. "I had to come really early this morning with my mom. The Looner was pretty strange, Cyril, pret-ty strange. She said she knew neither of us liked to lose, but if I moved to another class we'd have let this problem beat us. So we made a deal: we'll try to get along till Christmas. I have to do my homework and not bug her, and she has to let me come here and not bug me about my attitude. Then we'll see."

"So are you gonna do it?"

Maggie got her x-ray wizard look. "I don't know. It might be a trick. But if it isn't, I don't want her to beat me. Besides, it's good coming to the library. Mr. Huffer is fun. Know what we did this morning? Built card houses!"

An alarm bell started dinging in my head. Bald potatoes, I thought, how much did I blab? I pretended to straighten the books on a shelf. "Uh — what'd you, um — do that for?" I sounded like a mouse with hiccups.

"To find geometry shapes. Mr. Huffer said he heard that I liked building card houses."

"Ohhh … Yeah?" She was going to blast me to Mars any second now, I just knew it.

"Yup. Ms. McLean told him. She even knew about the world record. Amazing, Cyril. I'm going to have to figure out how she does it. Anyway, it was way better than boring old Looner Lessons."

Before she could say any more, the Looner and Mr. Huffer walked in. They called Maggie into the librarian's office. I leaned against the bookshelves until my legs had changed back from pudding. Did Maggie know I'd been blabbing? Was she teasing me or tricking me or what? I didn't *think* so, but I didn't want her all mad at me when I'd only been trying to help.

Then Mr. Huffer and the Looner were standing outside the library office. Maggie was behind them. Mr. Huffer said, "Cyril, this morning I got an idea from Maggie about how to raise money for the school's special-event fund. She tells me she got it from you."

I guess I looked kind of stunned because Mr. Huffer went on about how he knew Maggie and I had planned to go for a world's record in building a house of cards. He said it would be a big deal to the whole school if we shared it with them. The whole school would sign up sponsors and our class would do the building. Mr. Huffer is pretty roly-poly, and by the time he finished he was bouncing around like a balloon.

Maggie signalled me from behind their backs. She gave me the x-ray look and mouthed "Partners" at me. Suddenly I was buzzing like the fridge when the power went back on.

"Okay," I said — and we were trying for a world's record.

As soon as the teachers turned their backs, Maggie and I slapped hands. And that's the way it was.

Mr. Huffer told the class right before lunch. Everybody loved it, except for Russell. Nothing about Maggie was going to make *him* cheer. He didn't say anything though, just rolled his eyes as if it was boring baby stuff.

Then the Looner said she'd told Mr. Huffer that ours was the class to pick because everyone did BETTER THAN THEIR BEST, so she knew that we'd all be able to do this special project *and* our regular school work. Everybody groaned. Mr. Huffer laughed. "Way to cheerlead, Mrs. V." He left as the noon bell rang.

We got up, too, but the Looner made us sit down. She told Lucinda to close the door and stood there at the front, with her arms crossed, looking half like an army general and half like somebody's granny.

Then she said, "Yesterday I had to apologize to the teachers at the East Field Study Centre for the behaviour of my class, something I have never had to do before, in all my years of teaching."

She was really giving us the Venusian death rays over her glasses. It made you want to shrink down behind the kid in front of you, except everyone else was shrinking down, too. "The problems were caused by very few students. There was no excuse for their behaviour. Fortunately I can depend on most of you to do better than that. Monica, sit still."

I sneaked a quick look around. Most of the kids were ducking. I was practically under my desk. Russell was sitting up straight, the little browner. Bobby was trying not to giggle. Maggie was scratching at the top of her desk. Her knees were bouncing up and down.

"I'm not going to name names — Bobby, be quiet — except to say that Maggie should not have been blamed for one of the incidents she was involved in. Something unfortunate happened as a result. She has apologized to me and I have apologized to her. This does not excuse what she did do, but she should not have to take the blame for others."

Now the room got *really* quiet. Even Bobby stopped giggling. But Russell just sat there, smiling away as if the Looner was about to scratch him behind the ears. The Looner looked more like she thought we had fleas.

"There are few things more cowardly than letting someone else be punished for your actions, but I'm not going to take the matter any further. I hope the shame will be punishment enough for the others. They know who they are, perhaps we all do. But be warned: I do not intend to have to apologize to Mr. Huffer for the behaviour of *anyone* here. We were asked to build the house of cards because it was Cyril and Maggie's idea and because *I* promised you would all do BETTER THAN YOUR BEST. Now, are you going to do BETTER THAN YOUR BEST?"

"Yes, Mrs. V."

"Pardon?"

"YES, MRS. VEEE-EEE."

"Fine. You may go to lunch — QUIET-ly." The Looner reached for the monster purse and we were out of there.

At lunch we decided a whole bunch of stuff: that the Looner would never in a million years get any closer than that to saying she was wrong, that she couldn't have promised we'd do better than our best because Maggie and I never heard her say it, that we'd better not get Russell right now because it might mess up going for the world record if we got into more trouble, and that a tuna fish sandwich was a fair trade for peanut butter if you put a cookie in, too — which was how I got to make my first lunch trade all year, with Janice on sandwiches and Lester on drinks.

Mr. Huffer got the world-record project started the very next day. He got us rounding up packs of cards, made up sponsor sheets, and started us practising. We were going for the record the next Friday.

My book said the record was a house twenty-four storeys high, with 2,461 cards in it, so we were aiming for 2,500 cards. Mr. Huffer split us into teams of four. Mine was Maggie and me and Lester and Monica. On building day the teams would work on the card house ten minutes at a time. Mr. Huffer said that way everybody would get lots of turns and nobody would get careless. It was a good idea, too, because we knocked over a lot of card houses, practising.

Everything else got busier, too. Readathon ended the same day we were building. Old Lady Loony was working us like crazy. Even when we were building card houses she was always making us find triangles and penthouses and junk. Once we'd started bringing cards in, recess was totally different, too. The guys were pitching cards — you know, leaners and standers and covers — and somebody made up card tag for lunch-times. Crazy eights was mostly what Maggie did, with Monica and Stephanie and Janice.

After school we were busy getting sponsors. My dad signed up for a quarter cent a card, double if we broke the record. Maggie even got the Fenways to sign up for a tenth of a cent a card.

"How'd you do *that*?" I asked.

"I promised I wouldn't take the short way through their backyard any more."

The day before building day, we all went down to the library to see the big space we'd use on the carpet. Mr. Huffer was going to videotape us every so often and we'd all be in it, for proof. Our parents could come and watch, and the newspaper was coming, too. Then, when we were all excited, the Looner went blah blah blah about how we were going to be young ladies and gentlemen, and Mr. Huffer said he knew we were all ready. I guessed we were, too. Our last build that day we'd done 548 cards before George sneezed. On our way back to Room 9 Russell said he sure hoped *he* didn't have a cold tomorrow, heh, heh, heh. Russell was always tipping his team's houses over just to see them crash.

"Russell, if you even look at it the wrong way we'll turn you into crushed mushrooms," Monica said.

Russell said, "Yeah, right. I'm shaking in my boots, Moronica," but nobody laughed.

After school Maggie walked my way home. She hadn't done that in a long time. We crunched along through the leaves at the side of the road. For once, Old Lady Loony hadn't given us any homework, so there were no books to carry. Mainly we just talked about the world's record. Maggie said she thought my name should go in the book because it was my idea, no matter how many kids built it. I said hers should go in, too, because she made me get the idea.

When we got to my place, Maggie said she had to go right home. "I'm helping with dinner. We're eating early because my dad wants to take me to the mall tonight."

"What for?" I asked.

"Search me. It's supposed to be a secret. He's been wanting to do stuff with me lately but I haven't had time, you know? Anyway, I've got to go." She took off for my backyard.

"Hey," I called, "I thought you promised Fenways!"

"This doesn't count, Cyril. It's the last time." Then she was gone. I went inside and did some more practising.

The next morning I got just a teeny bit dressed up. My dad had checked that a photographer from his paper was coming for sure, so I combed my hair twice, then I ran all the way to school, doing speed shifts like a race-car driver.

Even the Looner didn't seem so bad that morning. Maybe it was just because there was no homework to check. Most of us even sang the anthem right out loud, and then our team headed down to the library. We lined up and Mr. Huffer videotaped Ms. McLean handing us the first deck of cards. Then we started building.

That first time down at the library was cinchy. The library carpet was perfect for standing cards on. We used up almost four packs in ten minutes. Maggie wanted to do more, but Karina and George and Steve and Debbie were already waiting at the door. We slapped hands with them on the way out and motored back to Room 9.

Old Lady Loony was making us do a thing about sound-alike words but nobody was really working. She had to tell us to be quiet about eight thousand times. Another team went down, then another and another. Just before recess, Ms. McLean came on the PA and said we'd used up more than seven hundred cards. We all cheered and another team headed for the library.

By lunch-time we'd gone twice more and used up 1,404 cards. We were more than halfway, Ms. McLean said on the PA. Everybody cheered again. When we went down for our third turn, I all at once understood how huge the house was going to be. Already it was twelve storeys high and bigger than one of the library tables. Just looking at it made me want to tiptoe. That was the first turn that my hands got sweaty. It wasn't so cinchy any more.

Mr. Huffer said "Half-hour break" at the lunch bell. Maggie went home because our team wouldn't have a turn again until school went back in. Down in the lunch room there were too many jokes about what would happen if somebody blew their nose too loud and about bombing runs with paper airplanes. I was sitting next to Janice Myers, and I took off outside with her as soon as she asked who wanted to play tag.

We ran around and yelled like crazy. Nearly everybody played, except for Russell and Lucinda. Russell was reading like crazy over by the swings, and Lucinda just sat there like a hair model or something. She joined in after a while, though. I guess running made her hair bob more than modelling did. Anyway, I never chased her.

When Maggie came back she was holding a book and looking around the school yard. Then I lost sight of her because George was chasing me and I had to take off. A couple of minutes later I saw her sitting on a swing a little down from Russell. The book was on the ground. A little after that we started up a new game and she joined in.

Back inside, Old Lady Loony gave us seat work: math puzzles and word-finder sheets, and we could colour our history maps or get out our writing folders. I tried to read for Readathon, but the closer it got to our turn in the library, the scareder I got. Then the group two before ours got back and we found out that Stephanie's hand had slipped and forty-seven cards fell down. For a second they'd thought the whole thing was going to crash. My stomach hit my toes and bounced back up to my ears. I saw myself reaching up with the final card, so high off the ground you could barely see the crowd below me, up on my tiptoes, reaching, the ladder wobbling, reaching —

"HAH!" *Bang*!

The card house exploded and I yelled. Everybody laughed. I was back in Room 9 and Old Lady Loony was saying, "Read quietly, Russell. There's no need to slap your desk. Back to work, everyone."

Russell opened his mouth, then stopped.

"Yes, Mrs. V," he said, as if he was really sorry. When the Looner turned away he leaned over the book again, folded down the page for a marker and slipped it inside his desk. Then he went over to the Readathon board and wrote another title on his list, a big smile on his face. I'd seen the book someplace before. I looked at Maggie but she was busy writing. I looked out the window and worried some more.

When we went down to the library the card house was seventeen storeys high. We put on nearly a whole pack, taking turns passing up cards and putting them on. Frozen tomatoes, were we careful. You had to stand on chairs now, and the caretakers had brought up ladders for later. As we left, Mr. Huffer wiped at his shiny face with his handkerchief and said we were less than a pack away from 2,000 cards. I saw myself doing that long reach up again and shuddered all the way back to class.

At twenty-two storeys, we were back. The ladders were up. "Two thousand, two hundred and fifty cards," said Mr. Huffer. He was keeping his handkerchief in his hand now. When the recess bell went we barely heard it.

At 2,400 cards, Ms. McLean came on the PA and called Room 9 down to the library. Mr. Huffer mopped his face and said that from here on we could watch and take turns till the end. The card house was taller than he was — twenty-four storeys high.

We sat down on the floor. It was quarter to three on a Friday, but no one was thinking about the weekend. We were sixty-one cards away from a world record. Nobody talked much, except once, when Monica wobbled on the ladder. We just watched, and waited for the Looner to touch us on the shoulder for our turn. At 2,430 cards, the library door opened softly and Ms. McLean came in. She held the door open after her. Squealing noises came from the hall, and Maggie's mom wheeled in the twins. Some other parents came in after her. Still nobody was talking. My turn came. I wiped my hands on my jeans and took two cards to make a leaner. I went up and put them in place. My insides fluttered a split second before the cards touched down but it went okay. The door opened again while I was coming down. It was my dad and the newspaper photographer. I waved and sat down.

Card number 2,450 went by, then 2,460. Bobby got to put on the tying card. He climbed up. It was an easy one, lying flat. He dropped it on and did a muscleman pose on the ladder. The photographer's camera clicked. We all laughed.

Mr. Huffer squished his handkerchief in one hand. "People, the next card breaks the world record. Since it was Cyril and Maggie's idea to do this, I'm going to ask them if they want to share this card or flip a coin to see who puts it on."

Everybody looked at us. Bobby said, "Maybe they could flip each other," and everybody laughed. Even Russell barked one out that sounded like Fenways' dog.

Maybe that's why I said, "Nah, that's the *short* way. We want to put on the *last* one."

"Number 2,500?" asked Mr. Huffer. "Are you sure? Can we go all the way?"

"Of course we can," Maggie said. She gave her Maple Avenue Marvel it's-cinchy shrug. "Better than our — well, you know." Everybody laughed one more time and Lester got to put on the first record breaker.

Two thousand four hundred and seventy went by

… eighty … ninety … ninety-five … Maggie stood up. "We'll do it from here," she said. I followed her to the table. Maggie picked up the last five cards and handed me two. Mr. Huffer helped her move one ladder around back, I climbed up the one in front and we stood looking at each other, across the top of the house of cards.

There was a flat space there where the twenty-seventh storey had been covered. I'd been hoping we could just lay the last cards flat, but it looked like other kids had been thinking the same thing. Every flat space was covered. I wiped my hands again.

Maggie puffed out her cheeks and said, "Okay, Cyril, five cards. I do a leaner, you cover the sides, and one goes on top. Ready?"

I nodded so fast my neck hurt, but it was better than trying to talk. Maggie lifted two cards. I squeezed the ladder as she flexed them till they curved a little, then she reached over and gently put them down in a leaner. A flat card slid out from underneath and the leaner fell over. More cards moved. I sucked in my breath. Maggie picked up the cards with the very tips of her fingers, her tongue pushing down on her bottom lip. Slowly she tried again. This time they stayed up.

She looked at me. I squashed the scaredness out of my brain, picked up a card, and put it across one open side of Maggie's leaner. It was so quiet you could hear the little click when it touched. I picked up the other card and put it in place on the far side. Click. I breathed again.

Maggie lifted up the last card and reached it out to me so I could hold it, too. Together we lowered it so it would be flat on the other four. I felt the weight leave my fingertips as it touched down, then my hand was easing back and it was done.

Everyone yelled at once. The flash from the camera went off and the twins started to cry. It all happened so fast I almost fell off the ladder. But I climbed down instead and the photographer took our picture and one of the house of cards standing there all huge and perfect. He wrote down my name and Maggie's. Then he started lining everybody up in front of the card house for another picture.

And that's when Russell screamed, "Wait!" Then he was jumping around waving the book I'd seen him reading before. "Twenty-five hundred isn't the world's record, it isn't even close! It says so right here. Cyril and Maggie lied! The real world record is 5,343. Look!" He jammed the open book under the Looner's nose. She put on her chopped-off glasses.

After a few seconds she looked at the cover of the book and said, "What — Mr. Huffer, what book do you have there?"

Mr. Huffer picked up my record book from the table and hurried over to Old Lady Loony. It got quiet all over again. "This is Cyril's, the revised edition. What have you got there?" He looked at the cover of Russell's book, too. "The *new* edition! Revised and updated with 350 additional records," he read out. "Uh-oh." He flipped open the covers of the two books. His lips were moving as his finger ran down the pages. When he looked up, his face had turned red. "Russell's right. We haven't broken the record. It *is* 5,343."

"See, I told you!" Russell shouted. "I told you they lied!" He was bouncing up and down as if he had rubber knees.

Mr. Huffer held up his hand. "Okay, Russell, that's enough. Nobody lied. Cyril's book says 2,461, but it's last year's book and I never thought to check and see if there was a new one. It's my fault, not Cyril's. Somebody's beaten us to it."

Everybody groaned so loud I thought the house of cards would blow over. Mr. Huffer said something about not feeling bad. Motormouth Russell was busy telling the world, especially the Looner, how he'd just read it two seconds ago and had to tell because it would be dishonest not to. He could barely keep the grin off his face. Liar, I thought. You found out way back in class when you yelled, but you waited till now to spoil everything, Maggie was staring at the floor. The carpet was gray — exactly the way I felt. All I could hear was Russell's weaselly voice going on and on about how surprised he was and how he always suspected something was wrong and it was too easy and he just wished he'd checked before.

Then I heard a voice snap, "Russell, *shut* — be quiet, Russell. Stop being a spoilsport. You've caused enough trouble already." It was the Looner's voice. My head boinged up so fast I almost lost my eyebrows. Old Lady Loony was giving Russell the proton disintegration beams like she wanted to turn him into a little pile of dust right there. Russell was staring back as if she'd just whacked him on the rear end with a ping-pong paddle.

Then Old Lady Loony turned to the rest of us and held up the book. "Boys and girls, it says here that this new record was set in England, so *I'm* willing to bet that our house of cards is a North American record. And if I'm not wrong, Mr. Huffer, we have also set a school record for the amount of money we've raised. Is that not right?"

Mr. Huffer said, "That's right, Mrs. V. A school record by far."

"Thank you. Here." Old Lady Loony dumped the book back at Russell without even looking at him. "Now the base of this card house is not big enough for us to add enough cards to break the real record, *but* I'm willing to bet something else: that this class could break that world record of 5,343 if they try again in June. A bigger house with a different design. Shall we do that?"

"YEAH!" we all shouted.

The Looner said, "You see, Mr. Huffer, I told you. This is a class that does better than its best." And then she smiled at us.

We left the house of cards standing for everyone else to see. The photographer said our photo would probably be in the paper anyway, the house of cards looked so neat. When he took the picture, Stephanie stuck her fingers up behind Russell's head. None of us said a word. We were being ladies and gentlemen.

We got back to class four minutes before last bell. Old Lady Loony said she'd total up the Readathon results for Monday, so if anyone had anything left to add to their lists they should do it now. I was still talking to Maggie about how it felt putting on that last card, but Maggie said, "Just a sec, Cyril."

She marched over to Russell's desk and grabbed the new record book out of his hands. Russell squawked. Maggie opened the back cover and pointed at something, then marched back.

"Had to get my book," she said, heading for the Readathon board. I started weaving around kids, trying to keep up. "I left it at the swings for Russell to find."

Then I knew where I'd seen the book. I caught up to her as she was writing the title on her list. Maggie said, "My dad took me to the mall and bought it for me last night. He said I should have a copy of the record we were breaking and then we'd buy the next book, too, with our names in it. That's when I found out we were wrong. But *I* didn't feel like getting everybody mad at me, so I let Russell spoil everything. Get it?"

From across the room I heard the Looner's voice: "Russell, *clam up*. I'm not telling you again."

"Besides," said Maggie, "we did get a record —"

"And in the newspaper," I said.

"And we'll get the *real* record in June, and —"

"Hey! Does that mean you'll stay in this class?"

Maggie stopped. "Hmmmm. I never thought of

that. I'll have to do some calculating, Cyril. But first I'm going to win the Readathon."

I looked at the board as Maggie finished writing down the record book. "Hey, wait, that only makes a tie. You and Russell have the same."

"No sweat, Cyril. There. The Marvel strikes again." Maggie finished writing one more title on her list. THE HOW-TO BOOK OF HOME HAIRCUTTING. Just seeing it made my hair prickle, now that enough had grown back to prickle.

Maggie said, "I saved this one just in case, Cyril. And now I win by one book." The bell rang as she said it.

The Looner called out not to forget homework. Everybody groaned one last time. Maggie was still reading the board. "Hey look at this, Cyril. You came third."

"I did? Hey —" But Maggie was already heading for her desk. I caught up as she said "... more important problems."

"Like what?"

Maggie was pulling out books to take home. "Like how Ms. McLean found out so much stuff about me. I even asked her and you know what she said?"

Suddenly I wanted to hide underneath my sneakers. Maggie didn't wait for me to answer.

"She said that there are some things principals just know and that instead of worrying about it I should go play with my friends. She said I had wonderful friends." She sounded as if that last part tasted bad. It did sound kind of yucky.

I said, "Oh yeah?" really cool, like, but my face was getting hot.

Maggie looked up from her books. "Nice beet imitation, Cyril. Hurry up, bozo, I've got to go." She gave me a little shove towards my desk. I wasn't sure, but I thought she was thanking me.

I got my books and my sponsor sheet. To change what we were talking about, I asked, "So what other important stuff do you want to do?"

Maggie said, "Well, I guess I could take care of your lunch problem."

That made me remember. "Oh, yeah." I coughed and kind of bounced on one foot for a second, like a sick stork. It felt like there was a tennis ball in my throat.

"Um, it's all done." I bounced on the other foot. "Remember the blackout when we went to the Centre? Our freezer went off for a whole day and all the frozen sandwiches melted and got wrecked. We had to throw them out. I make my own lunches now." Really, my mom and dad took turns helping, but Maggie didn't have to know about that.

For about half of one microsecond she looked surprised. Then Maggie said, "Just what I thought, Cyril. Remember what I said on the bus? About what else a blackout would do? No power? That's what I was talking about. And it's 'thawed,' not 'melted.' The Marvel strikes again, Cyril. No need to thank me, just throw money."

"Get out of here," I said. "Are you gonna say

you did the blackout, too?"

"Of course not," said Maggie. "I didn't have to, did I?" She led the way out the door. I rolled my eyes and followed her. Everyone was out in the hall, putting their boots on. "Don't worry, Cyril. You don't owe me for just a brilliant prediction. But you're going to owe me big if you still want help with yucko Lucinda Peebles."

"No way," I said. "I don't like her. She's dumb. I never liked her." I bent over to pull at my boot. It wouldn't go on.

"Like fun," said Maggie. "I thought you wanted to marry her."

"Gross potatoes." I was glad my boot was stuck. That way I didn't have to look at Maggie. I started to hop around on one foot again, pulling.

Maggie said, "Well that's good. Because Janice Myers really likes you, Cyril. Everybody knows."

I could feel the beet imitation starting again, as I fell over.

"Hey, Cyril, hurry up!" Lester called. "You playing or what?"

"Are you pitching cards?" asked Maggie.

"Yeah, what are you doing?"

"Crazy eights at Karina's." I could see the other girls waiting for her by the door. Janice was looking at me. We kind of smiled. I got a popcorn-with-butter-Saturday-afternoons feeling. "I'll call you tomorrow, maybe," Maggie was saying. "No, wait, I can't. I'm going out with my mom tomorrow and we're all going to my grandma's on Sunday. We could collect our sponsor money together next week maybe."

"Good," I said, " 'cause I'm busy, too. See ya later."

"See ya, Cyril."

Maggie headed for the girls. As I walked out to meet the guys I smoothed out my sponsor sheet and saw that my dad had written his pledge down wrong. Instead of a quarter cent a card, he'd written down 2.5 cents. I stopped and worked it out. It made $62.50. Doubled, for going all the way, it was $125. Wait till I told him. Wait till I told Maggie.

I looked up with my mouth already open, then stopped. Next week would be soon enough. Pitch cards now, collect pledges with Maggie next week. I'd spring it on her then. That left the whole weekend to think up the perfect lunch to trade with Janice Myers on Monday. I'd tell her about my dad's pledge, too. But first I had to figure out that lunch. It would be something new to think about, all the way home.

More Good Books

Maggie and Me

The first book in the *Maggie and Cyril* series

What mess could Maggie possibly get Cyril into next? Nothing has gone right for Cyril since Ugly Augie Crumley caught him riding a bike in a dress. Things get worse when Maggie convinces Cyril to trade his hockey practices for her piano lessons.

Cyril still has one hope left. The Christmas pageant is sure to straighten things out — isn't it?

More Good Books

Greenapple Street Blues

The second book in the *Maggie and Cyril* series

"But you can't move away," I said. "We have to do something!"

"I know, I'm working on it." Maggie didn't sound very hopeful. I crossed my fingers and tried to cross my toes, but deep down I didn't think even Maggie could fix this mess.

Cyril sometimes thinks life would be a lot easier without Maggie's schemes getting him into trouble, but he sure doesn't want her to move away forever. Everything's changing on Greenapple Street, and Maggie and Cyril want things to stay just the way they are.

More Good Books

Mushmouth and the Marvel

The third book in the *Maggie and Cyril* series

A whisper in class started it all — one whisper about a Valentine, and Cyril is almost engaged. But Cyril doesn't have time for mushy stuff, he's trying to get a spot on the TV-quiz-show team.

But who can a fellow turn to when he really needs help? Cyril's mom is busy at work, and his dad stays home writing books and scrubbing floors all day. Cyril doesn't want to, but it looks like his only hope is to ask Maggie for help.

Can Maggie save Cyril from marriage? Will Maggie make Cyril a TV star? Sure — as long as he does everything Maggie says.

More Good Books

Great Minds Think Alike

The fourth book in the *Maggie and Cyril* series

Maggie and Cyril have been friends forever. Maggie's rescued Cyril from some pretty mixed-up predicaments — she always comes through when he needs her.

But this time Maggie's not there when Cyril needs her — she's busy hanging out with Russell Hummaker, the class bully. Could she have a *crush* on him? Disgusting!

Will Maggie and Cyril's friendship survive the summer? Why can't things go back to the way they were?

Printed in Canada